PUPPETS FOR DREAMING AND SCHEMING

A PUPPET SOURCE BOOK

WRITTEN BY JUDY SIMS · ILLUSTRATED BY BEVERLY ARMSTRONG

The Learning Works

Credits:

The Instructor Publications, Inc., Dansville, New York, 14437, for use of a water cycle puppet play presented in *Puppets for All Grades,* © 1972.

Taplinger Publishing Company, Inc., for use of the movable witch mask which was inspired by the basic "smiler" pattern from *Paper People* by Michael Grater, © 1969.

Peer International, Inc., for the use of the poem "I Know an Old Lady" by Rose Bonne and Alan Mills.

Mae Canaga of Idea Merchants for use of the sock puppet construction method used in this book for "King Canine."

Grade Harp of Puppet Pals for use of the mouse house idea presented in her publication titled "How to Make Mouse Houses," © 1973.

Myrès Baré, scénariste de "La Clef des Champs" of Belgium for use of the story "The Bird" from which this book's puppet play called "Lisa and the Songbird" derived.

First edition originally published by Bruce Chessé.

The purchase of this book entitles the individual teacher to reproduce copies for use in the classroom.

The reproduction of any part for an entire school or school system or for commercial use is strictly prohibited.

Copyright © 1988
THE LEARNING WORKS, INC.
P. O. Box 6187
Santa Barbara, CA 93160
All rights reserved.
Printed in the United States of America.

CERTIFICATE OF PARTICIPATION

AWARDED TO _____

BY _____ ON _____

FOR _____

TABLE OF CONTENTS

INTRODUCTION

PUPPETRY TODAY

The ancient art of puppetry is very popular in today's world. We have become accustomed to seeing puppets perform on television, in shopping centers, and even at birthday parties. They are commonly displayed at craft shows and exhibits, and sold as toys and educational teaching aides.

Though traditional uses continue, we now find teachers, librarians, therapists, youth leaders, environmental and women's liberation groups, police departments, and even the United States Postal and Forest Services utilizing puppets to pass on messages and develop understandings. **There is no doubt that puppetry, in addition to its value as pure entertainment, is an effective tool for communicating and instructing.**

What do puppets offer that justifies their wide application and appeal? Basically, it is their unique ability to stimulate and enhance *imagination*. Everyday life situations can be transformed into new and exciting areas to explore for both performers and viewers alike.

CHILDREN AND PUPPETRY

How do children profit from puppetry? Though specific benefits for each child depend upon personal involvement in particular situations, there are many valuable outcomes which are generally recognized as good reasons for pursuing puppetry with children. Opportunities to experience puppetry often help children to:

- develop spontaneous oral expression
- improve speech, enunciation, and voice projection
- practice composition skills
- become more fluent in oral reading
- gain literature appreciation
- develop coordination and a sense of timing
- discover the joy of entertaining others
- gain self-confidence and personal satisfaction
- release fears, aggressions and frustrations in acceptable ways
- discover the need and methods for group cooperation
- understand and build interest in academic areas
- use craft, academic, and social skills in an integrated, purposeful way

In using puppetry with children, especially young children, keep the following suggestions in mind:

DINOSAUR DAYS Production Schedule

MONDAY Read story, make list of characters, design scenery

TUESDAY Make dinosaur stick puppets and background mural.

WEDNESDAY Distribute scripts, practice reading through play

THURSDAY Combine speaking parts with action on stage, add sound effects

FRIDAY Rehearse in morning, give show for first graders in afternoon

1. A child's first experience with puppets should be through improvised dramatic play.

2. A child's first structured experience in making a puppet should be through a very quick, simple, failure-proof method.

3. When working through a puppet project, plan completion steps along the way so that each phase ends with a sense of accomplishment.

4. Give children creative leeway in making and using puppets. Their imaginations will invent the best material for the end product.

5. When assisting children to perform, even on a very informal basis, help them to move and use their puppets and bodies so that the full benefit of the puppet experience can be realized by both the performers and the viewers.

6. When deciding on what to include in a puppet performance, remember that children like to enact everyday experiences, fairy tales, or other familiar stories.

7. Remember that it is difficult for a child to speak and move a puppet at the same time, especially if a script is being read. It might be helpful to have some children operate the puppets, while others who are situated where they can see the puppets speak the parts. Tape recording the puppet play in advance is a possibility, though this rules out some valuable improvisation.

8. Give careful thought to the purpose and time limitations for a puppet project before working with children. It may be best in some instances for children not to construct the puppets to be used.

USING THIS BOOK

Puppets for Dreaming and Scheming: A Puppet Source Book is written to assist adults who, for whatever reason, are seeking ways to use puppets that will add dimension and meaning to their work with children. A wide range of simple ideas are presented—from brief, incidental and spontaneous techniques to more specialized instructional and performance methods. As indicated by the chapter titles, the emphasis throughout this book is definitely on what to *do* with puppets.

In addition to specific uses for puppets, this book contains simple construction guidelines for the four basic puppet types: hand, shadow, rod, and string. Though inclusion of this variety was intentional, it is important to realize that *certain types of puppets are well suited to particular uses.* For example, a bird character that must fly is best made as a marionette. Furthermore, it is important to note the range of difficulty involved in each method of puppet construction presented in this book.

Puppets are versatile. Keep an open mind and *experiment* to discover how a puppet can change its voice, costume, or movement to become a different character to be used in a new way. For example, the bird marionette from Chapter Eleven could model an Easter bonnet in a musical parade or hatch from a speckled egg. If several birds are made, each could have whatever type of beak and feet are needed to eat and move in a way suited to particular species of birds.

The broad application of the contents of this book should not go unmentioned, though much is undoubtedly quite obvious. Chapter One, for example, contains a sequence of questions which should be answered before the stick puppet project is undertaken. These same questions can and indeed often *should* be applied to the other eleven chapters.

Many pages within this book contain patterns, scripts, directions, worksheets and study cards. *Under the copyright regulations stated on the credit page, these materials may be duplicated for direct use.* Some sets of directions have been deliberately composed for easy reading by children, and can be quickly arranged on a table with construction materials to create instant activity centers.

WITCH MASK PATTERN

Facilitating and directing children's uses of puppets is the major role required of adults for implementing the ideas presented within this book. Previous experience as a puppeteer is not necessary. However, practicing and developing some basic approaches to puppet presentation is *essential* in order to explore the full potential of puppetry, which is, after all, a *performing* art. Therefore, performance guidelines are provided as related to specific puppet use.

Basic suggestions for puppet production may be found in Appendix A, Behind-the-Scene Tips for Beginners in Puppetry: character development, manipulation, scenery, props and special effects. Appendix B shows a variety of simple stages for children to construct. Additional information on these topics is fully developed in many of the materials listed in Appendix E: Puppetry References.

Behind-the-Scene Tips for Beginners in Puppetry

STICK PUPPET PARADE
SKITS FOR ALL OCCASIONS

Stick puppets are one of the simplest types of puppets to construct and manipulate. A cut-out from a child's picture or coloring book, a paper doll, or any light-weight object can be attached to a stick. Rulers, pencils, popsicle sticks, wooden spoons, fly swatters, strips of cardboard, wooden dowels, or any type of long, narrow tubing can be used as handles for puppets. They can be attached by taping, gluing, clipping or stapling.

The range of characters for stick puppet use is *limitless*. Even a tooth character can talk and move, as indicated by this simple dialogue:

Permanent Tooth

Say, Baby Tooth, congratulations on no cavities! How did you manage that?

Baby Tooth

It wasn't hard, since Stephen brushed regularly to keep away my plaque enemies.

Permanent Tooth

How did it feel to have those fingers tugging at you all last week?

Baby Tooth

Well, Permanent Tooth, I was ready to come out to make room for your arrival, so I didn't mind a little help from Stephen.

Permanent Tooth

What will you be doing, now that I've taken your place on the mouth team?

Baby Tooth

Oh, I've been quite busy. First I was rescued from Stephen's apple. *Then* I got polished while sliding around in Stephen's back pocket. After a night under Stephen's pillow and a nice visit with the Tooth Fairy, I found my new home in Stephen's box of special things. I get my exercise moving from corner to corner, visiting with Katie Key, Ronald Rock, and all sorts of interesting characters.

A story such as this can take whatever direction is needed to suit the purpose at hand. Though dialogue may be prepared in advance, *spontaneous involvement* has particularly exciting and beneficial results. Frequently all that is required is forethought, mixed with a little ingenuity, and adult direction if children are to operate the puppets.

As you develop a skit, remember that the use of alliterated names—Lucy Lung, Gretta Grasshopper, Oliver Oakleaf—can add interest and personality to the characters. These names suggest a style of movement, voice, appearance, etc. appropriate for the puppet.

The following list suggests a variety of stick puppet characters to be used in dramatizing a range of topics:

HEALTH AND SAFETY

- red light and green light
- stop sign and yield sign
- table and chair
- knife and fork
- shoe and sock
- lung and heart
- car and pedestrian
- apple and candy bar

Amy Apple

Carl Candy

SOCIAL STUDIES

- happy face and sad face
- tall guy and short guy
- Brownie and Girl Scout
- country rat and city rat
- desert and rainforest
- longitude and latitude
- ocean and sea
- high altitude and sea level

SCIENCE

- Mother Nature and pollution
- sun (day) and moon (night)
- saltwater and freshwater
- raindrop and snowflake
- tadpole and frog
- butterfly and moth

LANGUAGE

- subject and predicate
- comma and period
- short vowel and long vowel
- quiet letter and noisy letter
- capital B and little b
- cursive *m* and manuscript m

MATH

- minus sign and plus sign
- square and circle
- straight line and crooked line
- inch and foot

MUSIC

- quarter note and whole note
- violin and bass
- piano and hand
- high note and low note

There is no need for an elaborate stage. Puppets can perform behind a bush, bench or table draped with a cloth, a movable screen or chart holder, or even a row of children! Glance at Appendix B for illustrated examples of performance structures.

THE WATER CYCLE
A COMPLETE STICK PUPPET PRODUCTION

The story of the water cycle is particularly simple to convert into a puppet play because the events are clearly sequenced and defined. There is no question about which puppet should appear or when a puppet is to enter or exit.

Besides dramatic expression and reinforcement of science concepts, an additional benefit to children in participating in this type of story enactment is application of thinking skills involved in the sequencing of events, so very important in developmental thought processes.

PLANNING THE "WATER CYCLE"

Prior to introducing children to the show, *make sure* they have had exposure to the science concepts within the study of the water cycle—particularly the term "water vapor." Children's science books and encyclopedias in addition to films and filmstrips contain lessons and experiments on this subject.

Before undertaking the play project with children, read through the remainder of this chapter, asking yourself the following questions:

1. *Is my major purpose in doing the play going to be a group dramatization experience focused on reinforcing the concepts in the water cycle?* If so, you will want to prepare a single large set of the seven stick puppets in advance of puppet play introduction.

2. *Do I want to use the puppets as a checking device to determine whether or not each child has grasped the concepts in the water cycle?* If so, you will probably want to duplicate the seven patterns in this chapter so that each child can quickly make his own set of puppets. This would *follow* total group participation using the large set of puppets mentioned in question one above.

3. *Is a major objective in carrying out this project to involve children in a creative art experience?* If so, you will want to let the children design and construct their own puppet characters instead of copying the ones provided in this book.

4. *Is it important that children learn to read the play?* If not, then memory of lines should not be required. Once familiar with the script, an adult or child can narrate the entire story for individual or group puppet performances. One benefit of this approach is that the puppeteers are required to do careful listening and can concentrate on good puppet manipulation. Of course, there are obvious advantages to having each child learn to tell the water cycle story in his own words, too.

5. *Is one of your goals to develop a level of performance perfection suitable to providing a puppet show for another group of children, or the families of the children involved?* If so, you will want to consider some production points listed in Appendix A of this book.

The above questions are aimed at helping an adult determine precisely how children will benefit as a result of this puppet project, and how much time to spend in carrying it out. From one to four 40-minute sessions may be necessary, depending on the extent of involvement. **All of the above items are important considerations which should enter into every puppet project that you undertake with children.**

INTRODUCING THE WATER CYCLE PLAY

Before any puppets are brought out or constructed, read the play to the children. Read it again, this time asking children to raise their hands when they think a new puppet character is indicated. Record the character names on a chalkboard or chart. [raindrop ☺]

Proceed with group dramatization of the play, *taking into account the responses to the questions presented earlier, and following the performance guidelines indicated in the script.* If the group is quite large, as in a school classroom, some children can perform while others participate as the audience, rehearse lines, or construct mini-puppets. Also, a few extra children can be incorporated into the play as puppeteers with the addition of more raindrop puppets, as noted in the script.

BUILDING THE CAST OF CHARACTERS

As children make their own individual sets of stick puppets, whether inventing their own designs or using those provided, the following construction steps are suggested:

1. **Outline** the shapes with black crayon or permanent marking pen.

2. **Add color** to the puppet characters.

3. **Cut out** the seven puppet shapes.

4. **Attach** the shapes to the seven sticks provided.

5. **Mark** the back of each puppet with its number in the story sequence.

6. **Write** the name or initials of puppeteer on the back of each puppet and on the script, if individual copies of the script are provided.

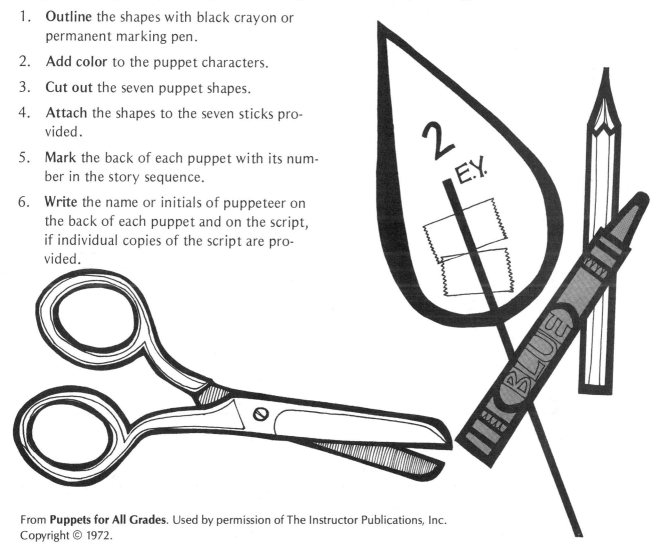

From **Puppets for All Grades**. Used by permission of The Instructor Publications, Inc. Copyright © 1972.

PREPARING TO PERFORM

As each child completes his set of puppets, he may be directed to practice on his own, perhaps with a script, following these steps:

1. Take a chair to a private spot.

2. Place your puppets face down on the seat of the chair according to the numbers.

3. Kneel behind the seat of the chair, using the back of the chair as a stage.

4. Practice by yourself, telling the story and moving the right puppet at the right time. (Refer to your script as needed.)

5. Invite a friend to watch. Take turns performing for one another, assisting where needed.

6. If you feel ready, ask an adult to come watch and listen to your "Water Cycle" performance.

THE WATER CYCLE
by Jerry

Before requiring individual performances, ask children to form a row or semi-circle with their chairs and participate in a group dramatization experience, using their own puppet sets in one or more of these ways:

a. All children move the appropriate puppet as the story is narrated.

b. A single child moves a puppet for the first story segment, the next child in the row does likewise for the following segment, and so on for the entire story. Each child can say his part of the story, or, again, the story can be narrated.

c. If the children have been required to learn to read or memorize the story lines as they appear in the script, they can recite together, moving their puppets in unison.

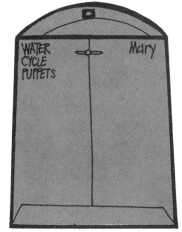

As a reward for learning the water cycle play, each child can take home his set of puppets, clipping them together with the script and putting them into an envelope for safekeeping. The child will hopefully want to perform with the puppets at home.

THE WATER CYCLE
A STICK PUPPET PLAY FOR YOUNG PUPPETEERS

PUPPETEER or ANNOUNCER says:

>The Name of this puppet play is The Water Cycle.

[Leaf puppet appears on stage.]

PUPPETEER, acting as NARRATOR, tells the story:

>Once upon a time, a little raindrop fell on a leaf.

[During "fell on a leaf," move the raindrop down from up high, onto the leaf.]

>It stayed on the leaf . . . until the sun came out.

[The sun puppet gradually rises. Sound and light effects can be added.]

>The sun warmed the little raindrop until it went away.

[Raindrop puppet slowly rises.]

>. . . and became water vapor.

[The raindrop has now finished rising, and has disappeared behind the water vapor puppet. The two puppets are held together, with only the water vapor showing to the audience. If there is a sky backdrop, the vapor should be the same color, so as to look as though it is not visible. If clear plastic water vapor has been constructed, then the raindrop puppet should not remain behind.]

>The water vapor was hidden in the air . . .

>Then the air cooled the vapor . . . *[air sound effects]* and it changed back into a raindrop.

[Remove water vapor puppet, exposing or returning the raindrop puppet.]

The little raindrop found its brother and sister raindrops . . . [If many separate raindrop puppets are in use, they appear now, clustering together.] . . . and all together they formed a fluffy white cloud.

[Fluffy white cloud puppet comes up to replace raindrop or cluster of raindrops.]

The cool air continued, so many more raindrops formed in the cloud.

[The dark raindrop cloud replaces the fluffy white cloud. Use sound effects to accompany motions of puppets, such as "Shhhhh" for wind. If many raindrop puppets are in use, they can return a few at a time in front of the darker cloud to make it appear darker and even darker.]

The cloud became very heavy, and it started to rain.

[If many raindrop puppets are in use, they can actually drop a few at a time, accompanied by the song "Raindrops Keep Falling on My Head" or faint pitter-patter sounds. Even if there are no extra raindrop puppets, a sound effect should be used.]

Then that first little raindrop . . . [raindrop puppet replaces cloud] . . . came back to earth . . . [earth puppet slowly rises from below as raindrop falls behind it] . . . and—would you believe—that little raindrop landed right on the very same leaf!

[Earth moves down, leaf with raindrop on it reappears.]

The End.

[Performer or group of performers rise and bow.]

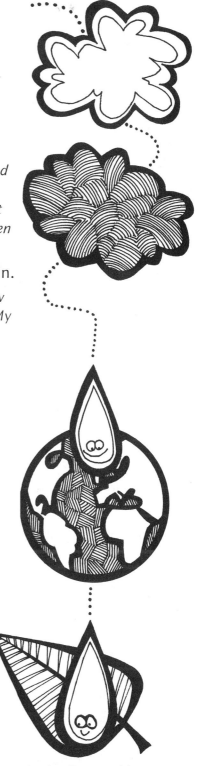

It is hoped that the detailed explanation for developing the Water Cycle play provides guidelines that can be adapted to a variety of other stories suitable for puppet production. Even the puppets in this chapter can perhaps be used in other ways, such as a story on water conservation and erosion which might be called "The Muddy Raindrop."

RAINDROP

SUN

RAIN CLOUD

FLUFFY
WHITE
CLOUD

THE
EARTH

LEAF

WATER VAPOR

THE GOBBLER
EGG CARTON MOVABLE MOUTH PUPPET

Gobblers are quickly made **junk puppets** that even four-year olds can construct within a few minutes. With little or no encouragement, interaction among puppet makers will occur almost immediately as the "big mouths" are being made. It is exciting to see children get right to the point of what puppetry is all about—*performing!*

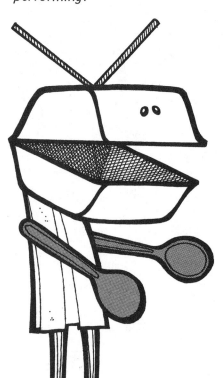

Egg cartons are easy to collect, and both the styrofoam and cardboard types work well for this project. Another source for gobblers is the hinged styrofoam boxes which many fast food restaurants use as take-out containers for their hamburgers. As these cartons and containers are brought in, *children should be complimented for helping to recycle materials* which would otherwise be used just once and then thrown away.

After the initial period of improvisation and experimentation during construction, children will benefit from some specific directions on how to use their puppets. Designate a spot as a puppet play area and ask children to take their puppets from cleaned-up work spots to this location. As children arrive, they can be organized by pairs, and puppet partners can interview, entertain, or mirror one another.

A simple stage might be used in conjunction with interviewing individual puppets. The success of these interviews in developing expressive puppeteers depends largely on types of questions asked. For example, questions which can be answered by a simple "yes" or "no" should be avoided. Instead, responses which require children to play roles, give descriptions, or offer explanations tend to result in more spontaneous and involved participation:

INTERVIEW STARTERS

- "Excuse me . . . may I please have a word with you?"
- "What is your name, please?"
- "What is your impression of _____?"
- "How did you celebrate your last birthday?"
- "What was the scariest thing that ever happened to you?"
- "What would you do if you were a tadpole that just broke your way out of your jelly-like egg sack?"
- "If you were a lion, would you rather be in a zoo or a circus? . . . Why?"
- "Would you please explain why the numerals one, one and zero—in that order—can make a bigger number than the same numerals ordered one, zero, then one?"

Additional questioning and improvisation techniques may be found in Chapter Three and in Appendix C. See Appendix B for simple stage construction ideas.

MAKING AN EGG CARTON "BIG MOUTH"

1. Use large scissors or a paper cutter to slice an egg carton into thirds. Each third can become a puppet mouth. Reinforce the hinge with masking tape to make a more durable puppet.

2. Help each puppet maker decide if his character needs the bumpy side up or down, as the holes for controlling the puppet will be placed in whatever is the top half of the puppet.

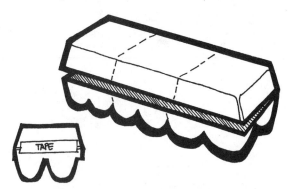

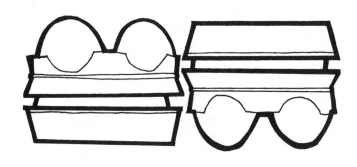

3. Demonstrate the possible uses of the small egg carton flaps. Individual children can then decide whether to cut them off or turn them into teeth or lips.

4. Poke and twist the point of closed scissors into the top, back part of each child's puppet, directly above the hinges. Finger holes made in this way last longer than if two circles are carefully cut out, because tearing is less likely. This step can be done as children are beginning to decorate their puppets.

5. Display a variety of odds and ends for making eyes, hair, ears, nose, etc. Styrofoam egg cartons are particularly good for poking in things like pipe cleaners and feathers. Pipe cleaners can also be used to attach things such as earrings or bows. Paper or cloth bodies can be stapled or taped to the puppet heads, though *puppet characters are often quite complete simply as heads!*

ADDITIONAL USES FOR GOBBLERS

SKILL WORK

As a child or his puppet correctly responds to a card held up by a drill partner, the puppet "gobbles" up the card. Different cards can depict *colors, clocks, symbols, math facts, textures, vowels, words, sentences,* or even *punctuation marks.*

A correct response can simply be reading and correctly answering exactly what is written on the card. More exciting involvement occurs when the responder must perform an action, such as pantomiming a phrase or manipulating objects or pieces of paper.

SOCIAL STUDIES

Puppets can become community helpers, historical personalities, news broadcasters, or characters in a folk tale.

DENTAL HEALTH

The flap of the carton can be cut and shaped to look like teeth. The result might be a "Bugs Bunny" or monster look, though anything showing teeth can be used for a study of teeth and dental hygiene.

MUSIC

Movable mouth puppets can sing in a humorous and exaggerated way. Songs like "Bill Grogan's Goat" work very well. Gobblers can also "mouth" the words to vocal recordings such as barbershop quartets or pop songs.

JACK IN THE BOX

POP-UP STICK PUPPET

Children enjoy the *suspense* that is built into a pop-up type puppet, whether watching it or actually operating it on their own. This pop-up is very simple, having a square instead of a cube for the box-shaped base.

Included in this chapter are a variety of pop-up puppet uses developed by adapting the following simple rhyme to different situations:

Jack in the Box
   Oh, so still,
Won't you pop up?
  "Yes, I will!"

Give a shy youngster the Jack in the Box puppet and see how gladly this child, once familiar with the verse, will volunteer the last line. Children will have fun taking turns, inventing different ways for the puppet to pop up.

When a child operates the puppet during an **interview session**, further participation is encouraged to suit any number of purposes. Questions can and should vary, depending on the child, the way the puppet pops up, the situation, and the desired focus of attention. Here are a few ideas for starting the **interview process**:

- "Hi, Jack, what's on your schedule for today?"

- "Goodness, Jack, what are you so excited about?"

- "Jack, tell me . . . Why do you think people _____ when they know they should _____?"

- "Jack, would you please tell me about _____?"
  (use child's name)

- "Jack, would you please tell me about _____'s favorite _____?"
  (sport, animal, etc.)

- "Jack, what is it that made _____
  (cleaning up, a name)
  so _____?"
  (difficult, a mood)

SHAPE RECOGNITION AND SIZE COMPARISON

If Jack is made with geometric shapes, as illustrated in this chapter, children will have fun locating parts of him that are specific shapes: *circle, rectangle, square, triangle, sphere.* An adult or Jack himself could ask:

- "What shape is the (my) box?"
- "What part (of me) is the largest circle?"
- "Where is the circle that is smaller than _____?"

THE "ANSWER BOX" JACK

If a number of Jacks are made with box fronts having different information (clear plastic pocket or card holder device would allow for changeable content), the child with the correct answer would respond to the following verse:

Jack in the Box,
With _____ to show,
Won't you pop up?
"Yes, here I go!"

SUGGESTIONS FOR "ANSWER BOX" CONTENTS:

colors	letters	leaves
shapes	numbers	clocks
signs	animals	food groups
words	seasons	math symbols

SHORT VOWEL CHECKUP

As the Jack in the Box verse contains all the short vowels as well as some other vowel sounds, a worksheet and follow-up puppet experience can be offered as an incentive to learning the short vowel sounds.

After reading and enjoying the poem, a child could be asked to mark the short vowels, perhaps being given the hint that there are eight short vowels to be found.

Upon correctly marking his own copy of the poem, a reward would be a turn to operate the puppet. Suggested Jack-in-the-Box uses for the child might include:

— asking riddles or telling jokes
— interviewing puppets or people
— delivering messages
— acting out the Jack in the Box poem with friends.

If assistance is provided, children can be offered the additional reward of making their own Jack in the Box.

The worksheet below may be duplicated, and is provided for evaluating a child's recognition of short vowel sounds.

FUN WITH SHORT VOWELS

NAME _____
DATE _____ SCORE _____

Read the poem to yourself. Read it again, listening for the short vowel sounds. Try to find eight and underline them.

Jack in the Box, Oh, so still, Won't you pop up? "Yes, I will!"

Now check your work with an adult. If you know the short vowels, you are ready for a turn with the Jack in the Box pop-up puppet. *Jack can ask for answers to riddles, tell jokes, make interviews, whisper messages, AND act out the poem above with friends.*

OTHER POP-UPS AND POEMS

The Jack in the Box poem can be changed in a number of other ways to accommodate different types of puppet characters, some of which are included within this book.

Bunny in your hole,
Oh, so quiet,
Won't you come up?
"Yes, I'll try it."

Bird in the nest
Wants to be fed,
He says, "Cheep, cheep!"
And pops up his head.

Here is a window,
Here is a house,
Knock on the door . . .
Here comes a mouse!

I see your shell,
Your tail and your feet.
When I see your head,
You'll be complete!

JACK·IN·THE·BOX CONSTRUCTION

Cut shapes for Jack out of felt cloth. Make his box plus extra head shape from heavy paper or cardboard. Tape or glue a skewer stick, pencil, or dowel to the back of his head. Finish his box to suit whatever use is planned for the puppet.

ADD YARN HAIR

BACK VIEW SHOWING STICK ATTACHED WITH TAPE HINGE

HAT

HEAD
CUT 1 FROM FELT, 1 FROM CARDBOARD. GLUE TOGETHER.

GLUE HEAD HERE

BODY

POMPOM FOR HAT

COLLAR·CUT FOUR

BOX

ATTACH BOX HERE

HECTOR THE DIRECTOR
ROD PUPPET PERSONALITY

Rod puppets are used throughout the world today, though their origin, as with shadow puppets, was the Far East. The traditional rod puppet, worked from below, is operated by manipulating three rods that extend from the puppet's head and forearms. There are, however, a wide range of rod puppet styles in use today ranging from a simple adaptation of the familiar hand puppet to a fully jointed and mechanized figure. Some large types require more than one puppeteer.

SIMPLE TWO-ROD ANIMAL PUPPET

PUPPET WITH ROD AND MOVABLE MOUTH

TAMBOURINE PUPPET PLAYS ITSELF

BOTH ARMS ARE ATTACHED TO A HEAVY BENT WIRE

TINY ROD FINGER PUPPET

LARGE PUPPET WITH CHILD INSIDE

LARGER-THAN-LIFE ROD PUPPET DESIGNED FOR MANIPULATION BY 2 OR 3 PEOPLE

CONSTRUCTING HECTOR THE DIRECTOR

The rod puppet construction shown for Hector on the next few pages results in a puppet character that expresses itself simply and clearly in front of a group. Arm and head movement can be well defined for effective directing or instructing.

MAKING THE HEAD

1. Insert and glue a cardboard tube into a three or four inch styrofoam ball. The size of the tube opening will depend on how many fingers will be placed into it as the puppet is operated.

2. Glue a piece of white felt over the cardboard tube where it extends out from the puppet's head.

3. If a particular skin color is desired, paint the complete head and neck and then set the head aside to dry. It is worth noting that acrylic paint works well on styrofoam.

4. Add the eyes, nose, and other features by pinning felt pieces, buttons, yarn and other odds and ends into place. Some items, such as pipe cleaners or feathers, are easily poked into styrofoam. Refer to Appendix A for a list of construction materials.

5. Complete Hector's head construction by adding hair. Adjust his features until he has an expression that suits his character. Since most of his features are only pinned into place, they can be easily changed at any time.

MAKING THE HANDS

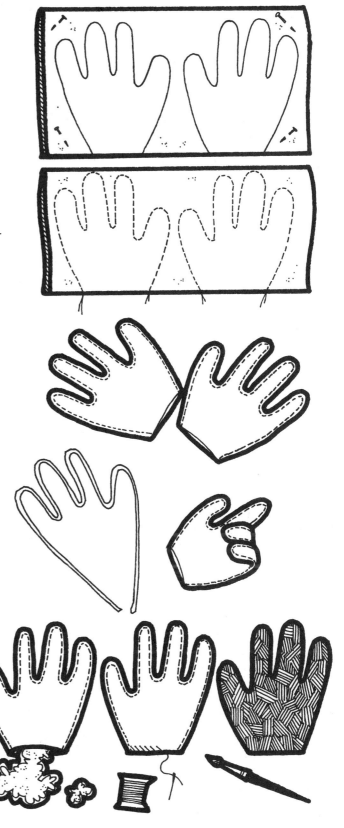

1. **Method A: Using a Child's Glove**
   Find a pair of very small children's gloves.

   Method B: Using a Pattern
   Fold an eight-inch square of felt in half.
   Trace the pattern provided and transfer this shape twice to the folded felt. Carbon paper may be used for the transferring of the pattern.
   Do not cut yet!
   Stitch along the lines you have drawn.
   Cut out the hands, leaving about an eighth-inch margin.

2. **Bend** a long piece of wire into the shape of the hand and then place it inside the puppet's hand. This will make it possible to change the hand positions as the puppet is used in different ways.

3. **Stuff** the hands by poking little pieces of cotton or polyester stuffing inside. Make the hand fairly firm.

4. **Stitch** up the ends of the glove to keep the stuffing in place.

5. If the head was painted, now paint the hands to match, and then set them aside to dry.

HECTOR'S HAND AND BODY PATTERNS

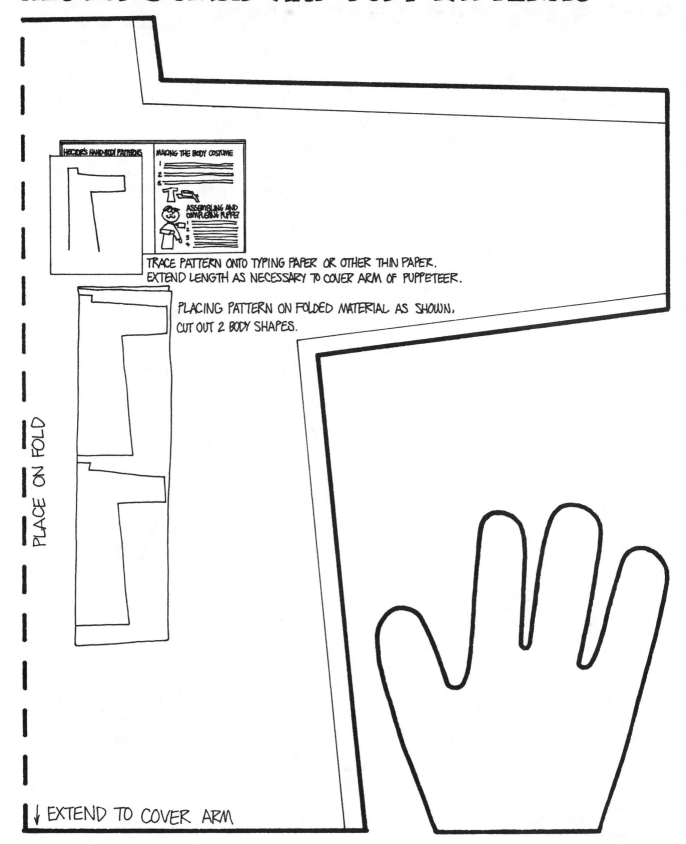

TRACE PATTERN ONTO TYPING PAPER OR OTHER THIN PAPER.
EXTEND LENGTH AS NECESSARY TO COVER ARM OF PUPPETEER.

PLACING PATTERN ON FOLDED MATERIAL AS SHOWN,
CUT OUT 2 BODY SHAPES.

PLACE ON FOLD

↓ EXTEND TO COVER ARM

MAKING THE BODY COSTUME

1. Using the pattern provided, cut out the body shape from whatever material is selected, altering the neck portion to fit the tube that was made for the puppet's head. The material should not be too heavy or stiff.

2. Hand or machine stitch the sides, right sides together.

3. Turn the body costume right side out. It might need to be pressed with an iron, depending on the fabric.

ASSEMBLING AND COMPLETING THE PUPPET

1. Attach the body costume to the puppet head by gluing and/or hand stitching the neck opening of the costume to the neck of the puppet. Make sure the front of the costume is facing the same direction as the puppet's face.

2. Carefully position the puppet's hands and pin them into place. Hand stitch them to the inside of the sleeves, "thumbs up."

3. Add whatever is desired to complete the puppet's costume and create the character—bow tie, vest, jacket with tails, artist's smock, hat, etc. A wand, paint brush, or pointer can be pinned into the puppet's hand. Sometimes doll clothes and accessories can be found for puppet use.

4. Attach a rod to each hand. A paper clip can be bent, attached to a rod, then stitched to the palm of the puppet's hand, as shown. Umbrella "ribs" make good rods because they already have holes for easy connecting. Heavy steel wire as used in coat hangers can be cut and looped at the ends to form rods. Taping a cloth or foam handle onto the end of the rod will make it safer and easier to operate.

PUTTING HECTOR TO WORK

Before using Hector with children, try to have definite character traits and voice patterns in mind for him. Make a list of adjectives that suit the personality that is hoped will be forthcoming. This will help to give Hector the Director speech and movement mannerisms which will be readily responded to by children. Of course, his character will not "come into full bloom" until he is interacting with children!

Here are a few suggestions on how to integrate a puppet character such as Hector into your group's activities:

As a music director, Hector can be operated by an adult or child for leading a song. His movements can indicate pitch and rhythm, and he can stop the singing or playing of instruments at any time, saying whatever is needed for improvement or cooperation, or making positive and humorous statements.

As a leader of events, Hector can direct a panel discussion, give directions, make announcements, tell jokes, comment on behavior, or ask questions. When used properly, he can encourage good child participation beyond what an adult working without him might expect. His use is suggested in other chapters within this book, including as a "mad scientist" in Chapter Ten, or a magician in Chapter Nine.

As a "master of ceremonies" for a quiz show, Hector can be the moderator for a group game called "Judge." This exciting game is played by following the procedures outlined below:

HOW TO PLAY "JUDGE"- A QUIZ SHOW GAME

1. A child is selected by Hector to play the role of **judge,** and is then requested to temporarily leave the room.

2. Another child is asked to play the part of **door keeper,** and will invite the judge to come and "take his chair" when all is ready.

3. A few **contestants** are invited by Hector to come and stand in front of boxed-off, numbered sections on a chalkboard, which are called "concentration boxes." There should be a piece of chalk and an eraser in each contestant's box.

4. Once all positions are taken, Hector starts the quiz show game. He begins by asking the participants at the chalkboard to respond *in writing* to the question he asks or problem he poses. He might say, for example, "Write the name of a living animal that is bigger than any dinosaur that ever walked on this earth."

5. Those at the chalkboard in the concentration boxes *must not converse,* and they should try to do their own private thinking without looking to one side or the other. The audience, of course, should remain silent.

6. The respondents or contestants are given a limited time in which to respond, and should return to their seats as their answers are completed or when Hector calls, "Time is up!"

7. When all contestants are seated, the door keeper invites the judge to return and "take his chair."

8. Hector must then carefully repeat the original question or problem just as he told it to the contestants. The judge must examine all the responses made, and decide which answer is the most correct. Of course, the spelling and neatness of handwriting for the word "whale" must be considered in the judging, as undoubtedly a number of the players have written the right answer.

9. When a winning answer is selected, the number of that answer box is called out by the judge, and the winning contestant immediately stands up to be congratulated by the audience and other participants.

10. The lucky winner now has a turn to be judge, and the current judge "steps down" to become the door keeper. Hector invites a new set of participants to be contestants at the chalkboard, and repeats the same "quiz show" procedure as completed above, using a different question, of course. The person who is winner at the time the quiz show must go "off the air" has the chance to be the judge the next time the program comes "on the air."

MOVABLE MASK
AN ANCIENT PUPPET FORM

Masks were used thousands of years ago by witch doctors, or shamans. In later years single masked dancers began to appear as performers. This ". . . was the beginning of theatrical performance and a stepping-off place for the mask to become a puppet."[1] Today large masks on human actors is a popular puppet technique in some parts of the world, such as in Poland. Masks are being utilized more and more by theater groups all over the world.

In its earliest ritualistic use, the hinged and jointed mask was placed directly down over the head. In later use it was moved off the head and held in front of the body. It is this later position in which the movable witch mask— the focus of this chapter—is to be operated. Nearly everyone will enjoy taking turns working and speaking with witch or wizard voices behind the mask in front of the group. The Halloween verse on the next page suggests one dramatic use for the movable witch mask: the witch puppeteer and audience or interviewer exchange lines.

[1] Bil Baird, *The Art of the Puppet*, p. 30.

Witch, witch, where do you fly?
   Under the clouds, over the sky.
Witch, witch, what do you eat?
   Little black apples from Hurricane Street.
Witch, witch, what do you drink?
   Vinegar, blacking, and good red ink.
Witch, witch, where do you sleep?
   Under the clouds, where the pillows are cheap!

MATERIALS AND EQUIPMENT NEEDED FOR WITCH MASK CONSTRUCTION

— 4 small brads

— 1 medium-sized rubber band

— a pipe cleaner or 8 inches of string or yarn

— scraps of yarn or fake fur for witch's hair

— a piece of heavy paper or thin cardboard

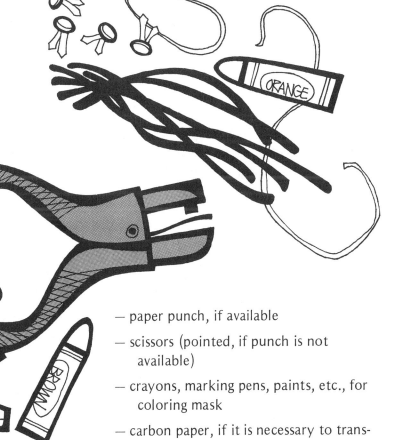

— paper punch, if available

— scissors (pointed, if punch is not available)

— crayons, marking pens, paints, etc., for coloring mask

— carbon paper, if it is necessary to transfer design

DIRECTIONS FOR CONSTRUCTING THE MASK

1. Make sure all materials needed to make mask are at hand.

2. Color in and decorate the five parts of the mask. 3-D objects, such as hair, may be added to the hat-nose piece.

3. Cut out the five mask pieces. Punch out or poke through the nine holes.

4. Put one brad into the hole on the hat; poke this same brad into the two #1 holes of the two eye pieces. Open the prongs, but keep the brad loose enough for easy movement of the mask.

5. Put the other three brads into place, matching holes that have the same number, looking at the illustrations to make sure you have the pieces going the right way.

6. Hook a rubber band behind the top and bottom brads (holes numbered one and four).

7. Now fasten the string or pipe cleaner around the bottom brad. This will make it easy for you to open the witch's mouth.

8. Practice working the puppet mask, holding it in front of your own face. It is fun to look into a mirror as you practice.

9. Practice the witch verse so that you can say it with your friends. Invent some other uses for the witch puppet.

10. You might want to try making your own mask design, such as a clown or old man. The witch mask was designed by a student who was inspired by the basic "smiler" mask pattern from *Paper People* by Michael Grater, Taplinger Publishing Company, 1969. This book has many ideas for paper masks.

WITCH MASK PATTERN

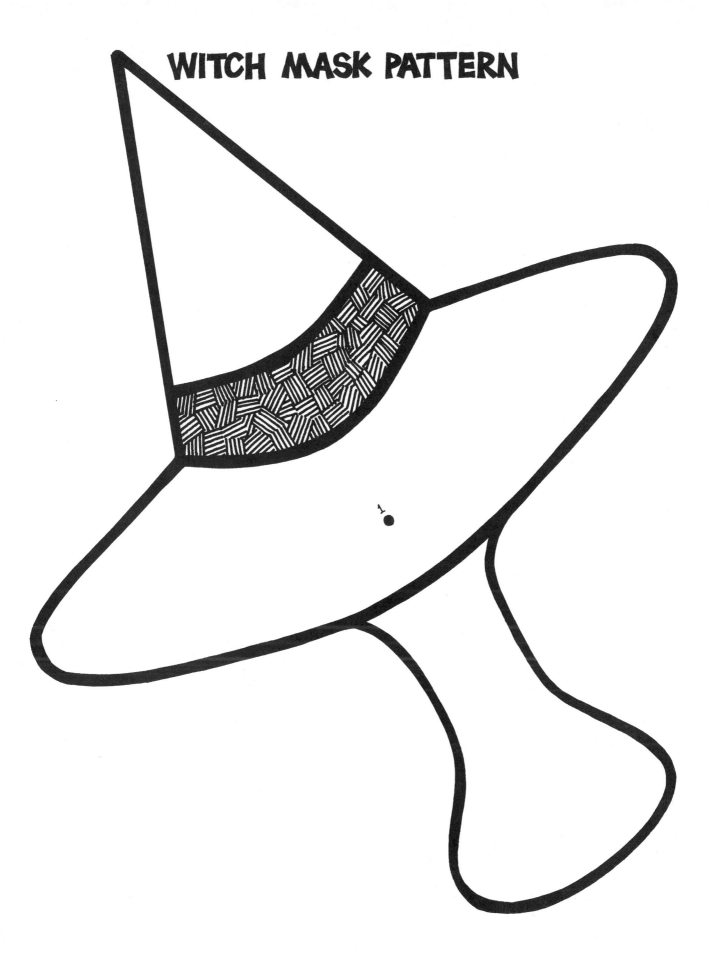

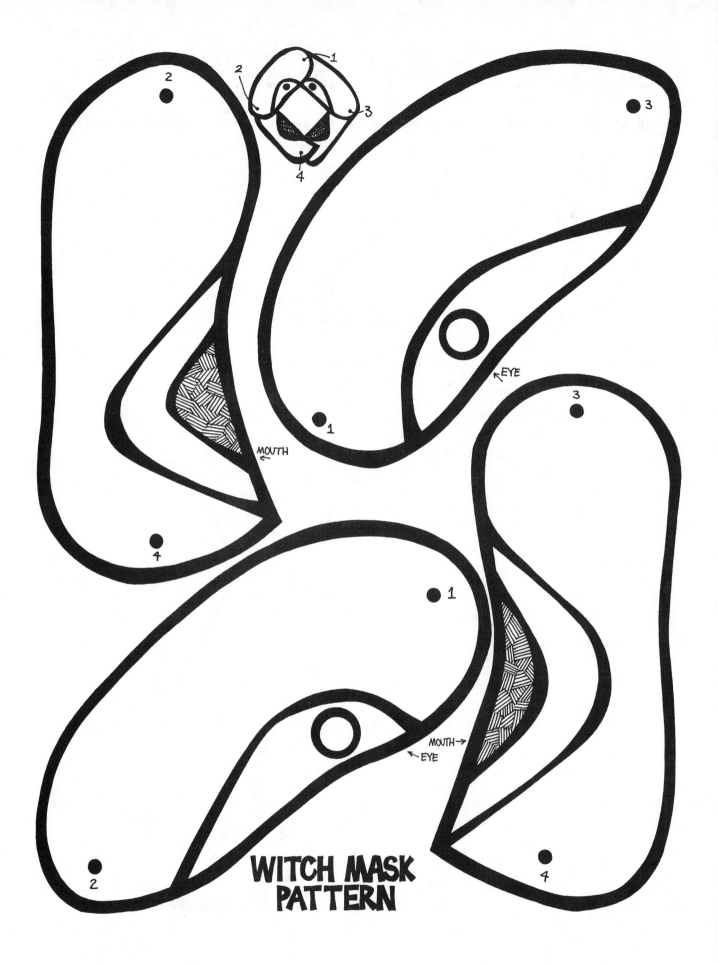

WITCH MASK
PATTERN

KING CANINE
SOCK PUPPET "SIDEKICK"

Because of his likeable and believable personality, King Canine draws instant attention and motivates children to focus on whatever is presented. His use in any of the following circumstances will generate excitement and an eagerness to participate:

- **as a greeter** to children as they enter a room, arrive at an event, exit from a bus, or join an activity

- **as an introducer** of a story, play, activity, visitor, or new member of the group

- **as an interviewer** of children or their puppets. He can find out about hobbies, favorite foods, reasons for conflicts or solutions to problems. This method can be used to check up on reading comprehension, listening habits, and understanding of math problems. For example, King might say to a child adding 38 plus 64:

    "Why did you stick that zero in between the one and the two?"

- **as a teacher** of a song or game, skill lesson, good manner, or anything that is important for a particular occasion. King can, in general, "impart wisdom"!

- **as a commentator** during a group sharing period or to individuals during or following involvement in independent tasks. This approach can be used to help maintain a standard of conduct:

    "Watch it, buddy! You know the right way to _____. Go back and give it a better try."

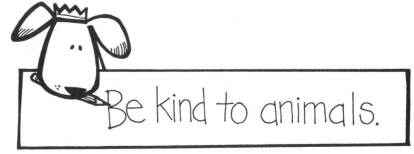

- **as an entertainer** who, in spite of having laryngitis, insists on singing or reciting a song, poem, story, or anything that is appropriate for the moment

- **as an announcer** who interrupts whenever an important announcement must be made or message given by King, "the royal subject." At an established time, King could be invited to make statements, such as reminders about what to take to or bring from home.

- **as a leader** of a birthday celebration or panel discussion, King could make a decree that "such and such" is to happen, or ask his "subjects" to perform in a particular way. This last use offers a simple method of evaluation.

In any of the above situations, a puppet resource such as King Canine can help an adult say and do things that may not otherwise feel comfortable or be possible. For example, King could faint upon seeing a horrible mess, or develop a pounding headache as a result of too much noise or rowdy behavior.

Children who cooperate or volunteer to participate in any of the ways described above can be rewarded by King. The following are ideas for rewards (the child and the situation would determine which approach would be most suitable:

- a lick on the cheek from King

- a chance to take King out for a walk

- "I decree that you may skip that last row of math problems."

- "I decree that your outstanding performance warrants early excuse to lunch."

CONSTRUCTION OF KING CANINE

The "stitch-in-a-mouth" sock puppet construction method is very popular and quite durable. The method outlined below is somewhat simpler, yet results in a very workable "mouth" puppet. It has been successfully made by hundreds of children of all ages and is suitable for a large group construction project.

Each child may be asked to bring a sock. On the other hand, large quantities can be obtained from laundromat lost and found boxes, rummage sales, or thrift shops.

MATERIALS NEEDED

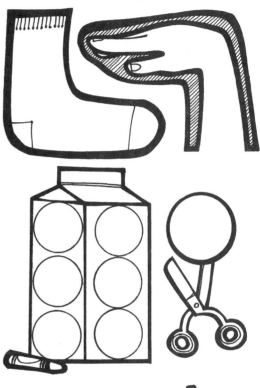

one sock
- Select one that is not 100% nylon, as nylon does not stick well in the gluing process.
- The sock should be small enough so that when the puppeteer's hand is inserted down to the toe, the heel coincides with the puppeteer's wrist.

one cardboard circle
- The size should be about three inches or ten centimeters across. The cardboard that milk cartons are made from is durable and can withstand repeated bends; other types of cardboard can be reinforced with tape.
- Once the basic construction technique has been learned, the size and shape of the cardboard piece can be varied to fit the character.

odds and ends
- Fur, pompons, sequins, felt, cloth, etc. can be used for eyes, nose, ears, tongue, eyebrows, costume, and crown.

white glue
- Preferably use heavy-duty craft glue, as this does not readily penetrate cloth and holds faster. Regular white glue that has been sitting out in a flat dish, or one that has been added to rubber cement in a four-to-one ratio will also work quite well.

MAKING THE PUPPET

1. Spread the glue with stick or finger onto the inside of the folded cardboard circle; set the circle down with the glued part facing you. Decide which side of the sock you want to be the surface of your puppet, and put this on the inside of your sock.

2. Flatten out the toe of the sock along the stitch line so that there are no wrinkles.

3. Place the center tip of the toe to the center glued side of the folded cardboard circle, gently pressing the toe down onto the bottom half of the circle.

4. Pinch the circle closed and gently pull the edges of the toe towards the fold of the circle, again making sure there are no wrinkles.

5. With your writing hand, pinch the cardboard circle at the fold. Hang on, and use your other hand to fold back the sock over your writing hand, turning the puppet right side out. Make sure the upper and lower mouth parts do not become glued together.

6. Remove the sock from your hand, allowing the mouth to dry while you plan and prepare the features and costume. For King you will need to make a crown.

7. Put the features in place by gluing them on. Some parts can be reinforced with a few stitches. Add costume details.

MOUSE HOUSES LEARNING WITH FINGER PUPPETS

Children have a natural fascination with small animals and their homes. That's why they will enjoy the mouse finger puppet and mouse house approach to puppeteering and learning.

This chapter introduces and develops a full range of mouse house designs and uses that complement educational goals for young children. Using the ideas presented on the next few pages, stories about daily routines and good habits can be dramatized and skills needed for reading and math can be reviewed. Teachers and their aides will discover that many of the strategies and topics presented can be easily integrated into ongoing classroom programs.

There are a variety of approaches to using mice puppets and houses which should be considered before working with a group of children on the learning activities described within this chapter:

1. **An adult can operate a mouse and mouse house for instructional or review purposes.** Children like to anticipate where the mouse will appear next, and will eagerly volunteer appropriate responses as requested by the adult or mouse.

    A child might be invited to come forward and use the mouse and/or mouse house in a specified way in front of the group.

2. **If children are to operate mice puppets, they can respond or perform individually, in pairs, small groups, or as one large group.** They can use their own house stages or ones specially provided that have been designed with a specific use in mind, such as math fact practice. For some occasions it might be fun to put several houses together to form a "mouse village."

    A single, large mouse house stage with multiple holes can be used by a number of children cooperating together during a free play activity period or under the direction of an adult.

No matter how mice and mouse houses are used, once puppet personalities are established and simple dramatization techniques are experienced, children will eagerly participate and will undoubtedly invent original uses for mice characters.

DRAMATIZING DAILY LIFE SITUATIONS

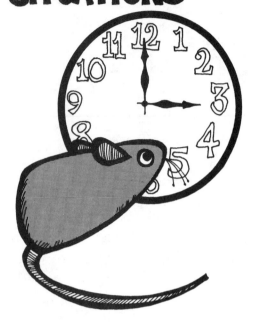

After children have enjoyed improvised play with mouse puppets and house stages, an adult can give some direction which will result in focusing or limiting the dramatization. For example, an adult could read or make up a story with lots of action involved. Children could move their puppets in and around their mouse houses, showing careful listening and interpretation of story content. New episodes would spontaneously come forth which could be used to extend this listening experience.

Children can also be given a set of circumstances around which to build their own stories. For example, they could use their puppets to act out a response to this statement: "Suppose your mouse puppet has just spotted a cat!"

A mouse that is operated by an adult leader can encourage children to contribute suggestions and make corrections. For example, "Heidi Mouse" can ask children for help in using the telephone, reading a clock, wearing appropriate clothing, or eating nutritious foods. Children who assist her have a good opportunity to practice manners, daily routines, and problem solving.

When the "adult as performer" approach is first tried, an adult who is new to puppeteering might understandably be a little reluctant to use a puppet voice, such as for "Heidi Mouse." It is often feared that an adult working in this way must perform as a ventriloquist. Quite the contrary is true, as young children are able to focus only on one thing at a time, which means they will most likely be so absorbed in watching the puppet that they are not really aware of an adult talking for the puppet.

There is a suggestion sometimes given to adults who need help in beginning to develop simple performance techniques for using puppets in a talking way with children. It involves pretending to have the puppet whisper what it has to say into the adult's ear. For example, an adult could hold "Heidi Mouse" up to an ear for a few seconds, nod, and then say, "Oh, I see. Well, I'll ask them. Boys and girls, Heidi Mouse wants to know what you think about her new door mat. Did anyone notice it? . . . What does it say?" The end result is that the puppet does some acting, but always communicates through the adult.

FOR AN ADULT NEW TO PUPPETEERING

There are limitations on how much the whispering technique can accomplish, as pointed out by the following dialogue which requires the adult to speak both for the puppet and for himself:

A BRIGHT NEW DAY FOR HEIDI MOUSE

Mouse: Ho, hum. *[Yawns, pokes her head out the second story window of her mouse house.]*

Adult: I feel like yawning, too. Why don't we all yawn with Heidi Mouse, and maybe that will help her to wake up!
[Adult yawns with children.]

Mouse: *[Yawns again.]* It must be time to rise out of my comfortable warm bed. *[Pokes her head out window.]* Goodness, the sun is bright today!

Adult: ___[Child's name]___, would you please hold weather puppet that will go with today's puppet show? *[Child selects sun stick puppet from among several weather stick puppets: white clouds, rain clouds, fog, etc.]*

Mouse: I guess I'd better get dressed. I wonder what clothes I should wear today? *[Goes back inside as if to look in clothes closet and drawers.]*

Adult: Raise your hand if you'd like to give Heidi Mouse some advice on what clothing would be appropriate for today's weather. *[Calls on several children.]*

Mouse: Oh, thank you, ___[mentions children's names]___, but I almost forgot! Today is my sister's birthday party! I think I'll wear my pink party dress.

Adult: ___[Calls on child]___, what would you wear if you were going to a birthday party today? *[Calls on several children while attaching a pink piece of cloth around Heidi.]*

Mouse: *[Pokes head out and looks at sun puppet.]* I sure hope the sun keeps shining brightly for my sister's party. Well, guess I'll go downstairs and fix my breakfast.

Adult: Let's use our hands on our laps to make the sound of Heidi going downstairs. *[Demonstrates and directs children.]*

Mouse: My goodness, this chocolate candy bar left over from Halloween sure tastes good!

Adult: ___[Calls on child.]___, You seem disturbed. Is something wrong? *[Asks for explanations and suggestions for good food.]*

Mouse: You're absolutely right, ___[children's names]___, *[Talks out of bottom story window.]* I was so hungry that I just nibbled on the first thing I saw without even thinking. Thank you, as I don't want to harm my important gnawing teeth. I'll just go inside my kitchen and fix myself some nice warm oatmeal. Then I should have plenty of energy to enjoy my sister's party! *[Goes inside.]*

It is important to sense the attention span limits of the children, and to stop with a comment such as, "Heidi, we've got to go now. May we come back tomorrow and hear all about your sister's birthday party?" or "We'll peek in on Heidi Mouse tomorrow and ask her about the birthday party." Your comment could stress a thought for children to ponder or remember, or a topic that will be emphasized at a later time.

PRACTICING ARITHMETIC

Mouse house holes labeled with numbers can be used for reviewing mathematical concepts. Different approaches for involving students and using special designs for mouse houses are explored in the math sections which follow.

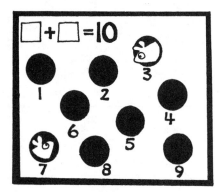

NUMBER RECOGNITION

Using a house with pockets next to each mouse hole, practice numeral reading, domino dot patterns, or number words. This same technique is readily used for recognition of shapes, coins, colors, etc.

MATH FACT PRACTICE

A numbered mouse hole can indicate a sum or a missing addend. Two mice used at once can show one of a number of possible pairs of addends for a given sum, or can request a response that is the sum.

SUBTRACTION HOUSE

For this math game a particular sum, such as five if the facts totaling five are currently being studied, should appear on the front of the mouse house, separate from the other numbers that appear by each mouse hole. As a mouse pokes through a numbered window, the responder subtracts that number from the sum and calls out the answer.

If two children are drilling one another and are taking turns with the mouse, then it helps to have the answers, which are the missing addends, recorded on the back side of the mouse house next to the appropriate hole. A simple, single sheet house could be made for each of the sums: four, five, six, etc. For more advanced children this idea could be adapted for use with multiplication and division.

The next few ideas require a mouse house designed with a long pocket or series of pockets positioned directly under a row of mouse holes.

NUMBER SEQUENCING

A card can be inserted into a pocket to show its proper place in a series, or several cards can be unscrambled within a large pocket. These procedures can be used for practicing letter or shape patterns, alphabetical order, or whatever type of sequencing is important for children to learn.

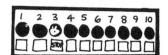

PLACE VALUE

Each window is used for one digit's place, and interchangeable number cards are used in the pockets by each window. The mouse pops out and the child tells whether ones, tens, hundreds, or thousands is indicated. For beginning learners, it would be a good idea to accompany the reading of the numbers with the manipulating of whatever counting materials are used for place value. The mouse could try to fool children: "You tell me that this window is worth five hundred, but I only see a five!"

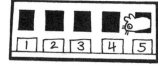

NUMBER LINE

A mouse can help children learn how to solve equations, such as 1 + 2 = □, by using a house with a long series of numbered mouse holes. Word cards saying "start" or "go" or "end" or "stop", color coded red and green, can be inserted into the pocket that holds the appropriate number. Moves on the line can be made by the mouse, who can count aloud as he pokes his head through one window after another, in sequence.

TELLING TIME

A clock-shaped mouse house can motivate the study of telling time. An adult can operate a single clock house in front of a group, or ask children to respond to a question using their own house clocks and mice.

A mouse peering through the appropriate clock hole can be used to show any of the following:

- the little hand's (hour hand's) place at three o'clock
- the big hand's (minute hand's) place at three o'clock
- the big hand's place at 20 minutes past the hour
- the big hand's place at five minutes before the hour
- the hour closest to bedtime

PHONICS AND LANGUAGE SKILLS

By placing cards into pockets that are situated next to individual mouse holes, numerous opportunities exist for practicing phonics and language skills.

Children can respond orally or with their own mouse and mouse house to indicate answers for any of the following topics:

- short and long vowel sounds
- parts of sentences — *who, when, where, what, why, how*
- parts of speech — *verb, noun, pronoun, etc.*
- word families — ___ark, ___old, ___ate, etc.
- beginning or ending sounds, including blends *(bl, sp, gr)* or digraphs *(ch, sh, th)*
- suffixes or prefixes
- the number of syllables heard in a word

A child "playing teacher" or an adult can poke a mouse through a hole and call on someone to give a response, such as a word with the short vowel "a." One advantage of all children in the group having identical mouse houses is that the adult can quickly scan all the responses to determine how well individual children are understanding the concepts.

If a basic mouse house design is duplicated, such as one with vowels written by each of five mouse holes, children can decorate and cut out the windows to make their own mouse house in preparation for individual or group practice sessions. The full-scale patterns pictured in this chapter are intended for this possible use.

OTHER USES

1. **Use a mouse to give directions** on where a child should place his body, hand, finger, or mouse. Here's a poem young children will enjoy as they operate a mouse puppet:

MY MOUSE

Mouse is looking all around.
Mouse is sniffing on the ground.
Mouse is sleeping in her bed.
Mouse is sitting on my head.
Mouse is looking at my toes.
Mouse can kiss me on the nose.
Mouse can whisper in my ear.
What's she saying? Can you hear?
Mouse can go and hide behind me.
Wherever I go my mouse can find me.

—by Beverly Armstrong

2. **A mouse can ask questions or make comments** from a mouse house window before, during or after the reading of a story. This technique can be used to check listening habits, comprehension skills, or simply to encourage children to speak up and relate their thoughts about a story event.

3. **An adult can walk around the group with the mouse,** making comments to children as they go about tasks or listening to individual children read. As carrying around a mouse house could be cumbersome, a little nest made with the other hand can be used as a simple stage.

4. **A mouse can be used to motivate children to write creatively** by introducing an idea like, "What it's Like to be Chased by a Cat," "Garbage Can Treasures," or "When the Bulldozer Demolished My Home." Instead of talking from a mouse house, it would be more appropriate for this mouse to talk from a nest, which can be made from burlap, straw, raffia, or shredded paper.

5. **Provide a regular special time when children can talk** with "Heidi Mouse" by ringing her doorbell or knocking on her door. She can answer questions, listen to concerns, give advice, or even make announcements and give reminders. She might also have responses to notes or letters left for her at a previous time. (See the letter writing form suggested on page 71 of this book.)

VISITORS
WELCOME
2-2:15 P.M.
TUESDAYS AND
THURSDAYS

MOUSE HOUSE DESIGNS

Before making a mouse house, first consider how it will be *used*, as the house construction method or design is in some instances determined by specific types of uses. For example, a long row of evenly spaced holes is needed for the number line practice house. In addition to the style of mouse house to be made, the positions in which the house will be operated should be considered. The construction of the house will partially depend upon how the house will be held in relationship to the puppeteer:

On a Table or Desk Top, a Ledge or Bench

A mouse house to be used in this fashion should be built so as to be free standing if it is to be frequently used by the same person or if several puppeteers will be using it at the same time. A self-supporting stage leaves both of the puppeteer's hands free to handle puppets and other objects.

Held in One Hand to the Side or in Front of the Body

Either a free-standing box-type stage or a flat stage made of fairly durable material can be operated in these positions. One of the puppeteer's hands will always be holding up the stage.

Perched on a Lap

Again, either form of mouse house is workable, depending on the importance to the puppeteer of having a free hand. The house can be made to stand up on a lap if a strap is placed from one side to the other and goes around behind the neck of the operator.

MOUSE HOUSE CONSTRUCTION

BOX FLAP ↗

Mouse house designs can be drawn right onto the mouse house stage. If the plan is on a piece of paper, this can be attached directly to the house. Mouse houses can be made from a paper bag, box, heavy sheet of paper or cardboard, masonite, or even plywood. Extra reinforcement may be necessary. Odds and ends of yardage, fringe, plastic flowers, etc.,can be added to give a "Three-D" effect, though this makes storage of mouse houses less efficient.

One clever adult carved mouse holes into a dried loaf of Italian bread and then sprayed it to make it look like a piece of cheese. This points out the endless source of materials that can be used for building mouse houses.

"MULTIPLE USE" HOUSE CONSTRUCTION

For multiple uses of a single mouse house—as for creative play situation stories, number drill, or classification practice—the following construction ideas should be noted:

Flannel cloth can be used to face a house made from styrofoam or sound board. This allows for the use of existing and newly made flannel board materials and makes possible the use of any object that can be pinned onto the board—a flowery prop, letter, number, word, additional character, etc.

Pockets can be made next to each mouse hole in such a way as to allow for easy change of contents. If these pockets are made with clear plastic (acetate), they not only serve to hold and protect a card but provide an erasable writing surface for crayons or grease pencils. Double sticky tape and contact paper can come in handy during the construction.

BEND TOP OF CARD FORWARD FOR EASIER HANDLING.

In addition to the mouse house designs shown thus far, the three pages that follow depict houses that may be reproduced and glued to boxes or cardboard to make mouse house stages. Here is a brief description of each house in terms of suggested uses:

The "This or That" House

This simplified house has only two holes for many types of responses: *yes, no; true, false; left, right; happy, sad; beginning, ending sounds; parts of a story, portion of the alphabet,* etc.

The "Conversation" House

With an upstairs and downstairs, this house is designed for creative play and dramatizing life situations and stories.

The "Answer Box" House

Places are marked for making five card pockets, one next to each hole. Changeable cards can show animal or food groups, the five senses, etc.

CUT OUT WINDOW

CUT OUT WINDOW

THE "CONVERSATION HOUSE"

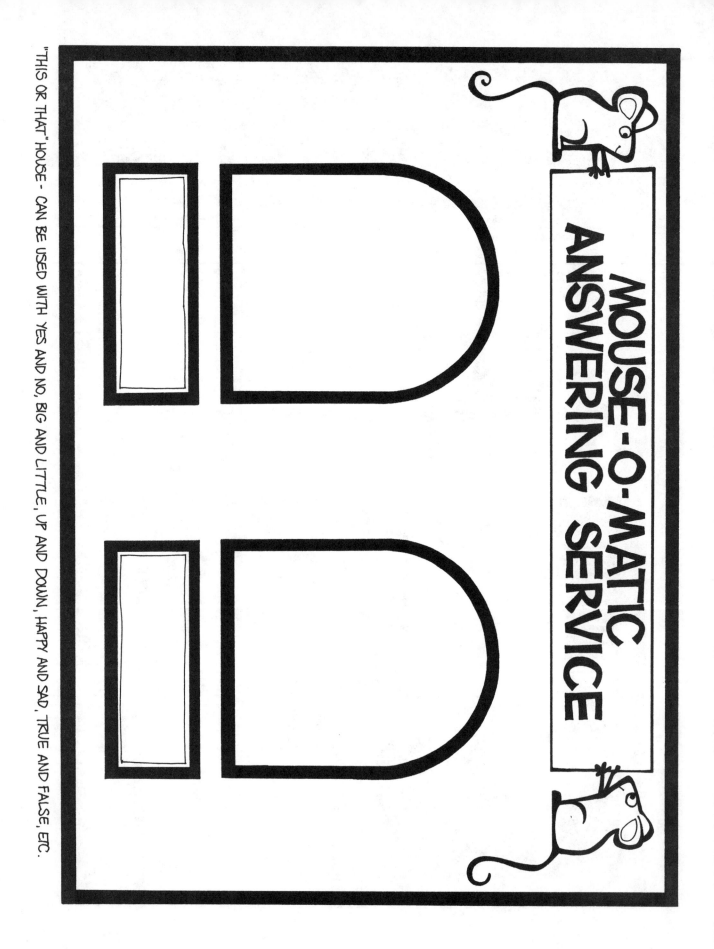

"THIS OR THAT" HOUSE - CAN BE USED WITH YES AND NO, BIG AND LITTLE, UP AND DOWN, HAPPY AND SAD, TRUE AND FALSE, ETC.

MOUSE-O-MATIC ANSWERING SERVICE

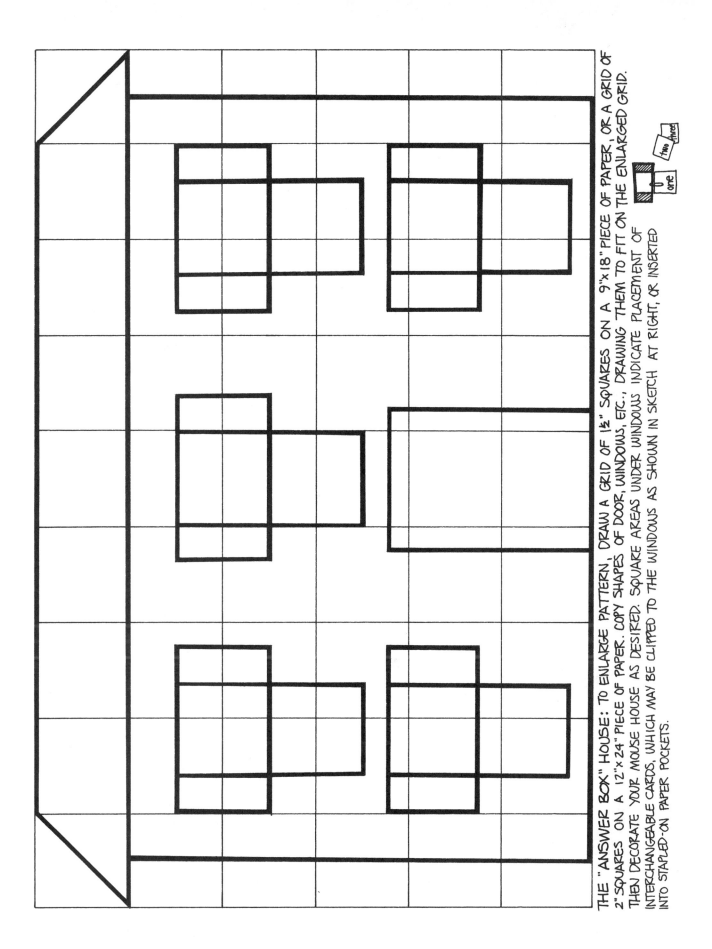

THE "ANSWER BOX" HOUSE: TO ENLARGE PATTERN, DRAW A GRID OF 1½" SQUARES ON A 9"x18" PIECE OF PAPER, OR A GRID OF 2" SQUARES ON A 12"x24" PIECE OF PAPER. COPY SHAPES OF DOOR, WINDOWS, ETC., DRAWING THEM TO FIT ON THE ENLARGED GRID. THEN DECORATE YOUR MOUSE HOUSE AS DESIRED. SQUARE AREAS UNDER WINDOWS INDICATE PLACEMENT OF INTERCHANGEABLE CARDS, WHICH MAY BE CLIPPED TO THE WINDOWS AS SHOWN IN SKETCH AT RIGHT, OR INSERTED INTO STAPLED-ON PAPER POCKETS.

a	what?	first last
e	where? why?	yes
i	when?	no who?
o	how?	
u		

meat	fish	—ink
fruit and vegetable	amphibian	—and
milk	reptile	—ent
cereal and bread	bird	—ock
extra	mammal	—ug

MOUSE PUPPET CONSTRUCTION METHODS

Four types of mouse puppet construction are presented to suit different ages, abilities and situations:

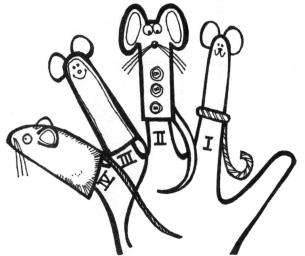

TYPE I — "The Finger Mouse" . . . is very temporary, made quickly from simple materials.

TYPE II — "Tube Type Finger Puppet" . . . the body shape is formed by a cloth or paper cylinder.

TYPE III — "Glove Finger Mouse" is made from a finger of a glove; is quite durable, as is Type II.

TYPE IV — "Fuzzy Plush Mouse" closely resembles a real mouse. "Mass mice" production instructions are included.

TYPE I· THE FINGER MOUSE

Glue paper or cloth ears to the fingernail of the first finger of the writing hand. Add the features with cosmetic pencils and water-based marking pens. A piece of string, yarn, or pipe cleaner can be tied around the finger to form a tail.

TYPE II· TUBE TYPE FINGER PUPPET

Transfer the pattern provided to paper or felt. It should be glued or stitched to form a cylinder after being fitted to the puppeteer's finger. Features and other details can then be added.

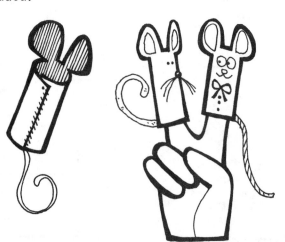

MAY BE MADE
HORIZONTALLY
OR VERTICALLY

TYPE III·GLOVE FINGER MOUSE

Snip a finger off of an old glove made of a material that will not ravel. Glue or stitch the features onto this mouse body. (Gloves are generally available at rummage sales and thrift shops.)

TYPE IV·FUZZY PLUSH MOUSE

MATERIALS NEEDED:

body: non-ravel fuzzy material

ears: felt or leather scraps

eyes/nose: small sequins, beads, or buttons

whiskers: heavy thread

EQUIPMENT NEEDED:

needle   thread
scissors   pins
pencil, newsprint and carbon paper for pattern transfer
sewing machine (optional)
heavy-duty craft glue

INSTRUCTIONS

1. Transfer the mouse body pattern to newsprint using carbon paper and a pencil.

2. Cut out the pattern piece and pin it to the back side of the fuzzy material. Cut out the mouse's fuzzy body shape.

3. Fold the body piece in half starting at the nose, making sure the fuzzy side of the material is on the *inside.*

4. Stitch up the body and turn it right side out. Poke out the nose with the point of closed scissors.

5. Cut out the ears and tail. Hold them in several different positions before deciding where to place them.

6. Glue or stitch the ears and tail into place.

7. Use a needle and thread to attach sequins, buttons, or beads for the eyes and nose.

8. Add the whiskers by stitching back and forth on either side of the nose with heavy-duty thread. Tie the whiskers together to hold them in place, making knots where they come out by the nose. If fine telephone wire is available, small pieces can be used in place of the thread. They can be poked in and then glued in place at the nose.

9. *Optional:* turn the open end of the mouse up into the inside of the body just a little, and glue or stitch it into place.

10. Let the glue dry before playing with the mouse puppet.

Note: The mouse's eyes could be the movable ones from a hobby store. These and other features could be glued into place, thereby avoiding stitching which is difficult for young children.

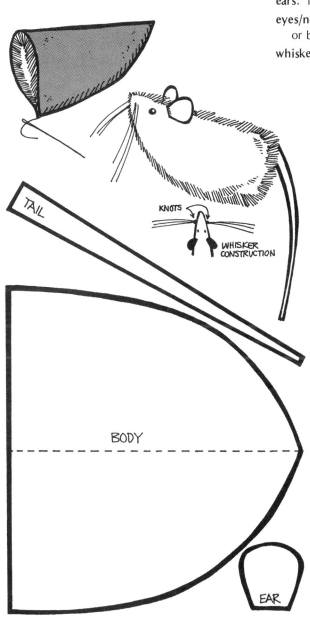

TAIL

KNOTS

WHISKER CONSTRUCTION

BODY

EAR

MASS MICE PRODUCTION

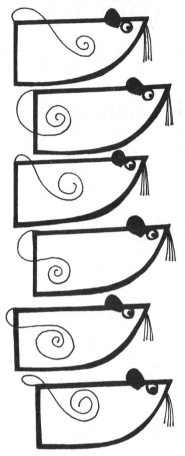

Transfer the mouse body pattern onto cardboard or heavy paper. Then carefully cut it out. Cut long strips of mouse material that are *at least* one-half inch wider than the width of the mouse pattern. Fold the cloth strip lengthwise, *fuzzy side in*. Fold and cut the body pattern and use a marking pen to transfer this shape to the material. Stitch along the lines, being sure to anchor the thread at each end of every mouse puppet.

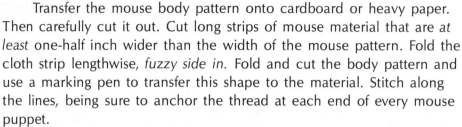

Cut the mice apart from one another, being careful not to cut the knotted thread. Trim the excess cloth near the curves, then turn the mouse bodies right side out. It is easy to poke out the nose with the point of closed scissors or a dull pencil.

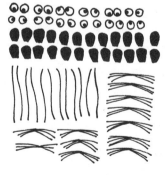

Depending on the situation, individuals can add the features and complete the mouse, following directions five through ten on the previous page.

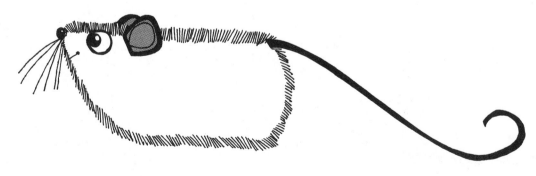

CREEPY CATERPILLAR

VERSATILE ROD PUPPET

Original ideas for making and using this simple rod puppet will emerge following its introduction, which should include presenting an interesting variety of construction materials and encouraging exploration of all possible puppet movements.

Through adult direction or child selection, this two-rodded puppet form can become a **caterpillar, dragon,** or **worm** character, such as "Book Worm Willie."

The construction steps that are basic to building any of these creatures are clearly presented in outline fashion so that children can be provided with an opportunity to read or follow the directions independently or with minimal adult guidance.

Since this creature can take on any one of a variety of puppet personalities, there are many options to consider when deciding how its use might be incorporated into group work to provide valuable and creative learning experiences for children.

The following "idea list" includes a number of specific educational uses as well as other suggestions which can be helpful in determining how the advantages of this rod puppet can be realized.

THE STORY OF LAZY DAISY

IF MADE AS A WORM, THIS PUPPET CAN...

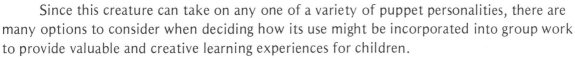

- be a "word worm" that helps children figure out and learn new words.

- be a "book worm" who relates interesting reading experiences and interviews children about the books they've read.

- be a "worry worm" who finds it necessary to frequently "check out the scene," giving reminders and making announcements to help children learn about important things.

- come out into the forest "litter" at night, telling how it helps to keep the soil rich and fresh, and what it notices about other animals that come out at night.

- tell how it got "flooded out" by a recent rain.

IF MADE AS A CATERPILLAR, IT CAN...

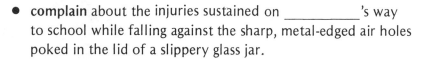

- **tell** how it *feels* to be dropped and carried around in a glass jar, then returned "home" just before starving.

- **complain** about the injuries sustained on _____'s way to school while falling against the sharp, metal-edged air holes poked in the lid of a slippery glass jar.

- **pretend** to munch on vegetation, and tell what it is like to be a newly-hatched, hungry insect that will grow up to be several times its existing size in a matter of only a few weeks.

- **relate** incidents that happened while searching to find a good place to form its cocoon, pointing out the natural "hazards" faced by caterpillars, such as being eaten by a lizard.

- **help** children to better understand the miraculous sequence of events that will occur as it changes into a moth or butterfly.

- **reminisce** about some "unusual events" of the past two weeks: hatching in Mr. McGregor's garden, narrowly escaping Peter Rabbit's mouth, catching a cold in Mrs. McGregor's refrigerator, nearly suffocating in her garbage can, then feasting in the compost pile while preparing for the big change to come.

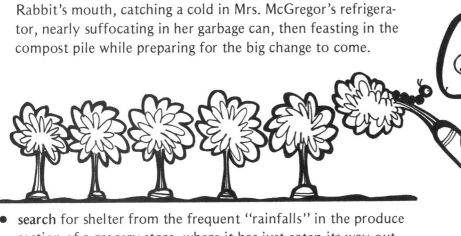

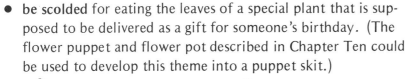

- **search** for shelter from the frequent "rainfalls" in the produce section of a grocery store, where it has just eaten its way out of a head of lettuce and is about to be noticed by a customer!

- **be scolded** for eating the leaves of a special plant that is supposed to be delivered as a gift for someone's birthday. (The flower puppet and flower pot described in Chapter Ten could be used to develop this theme into a puppet skit.)

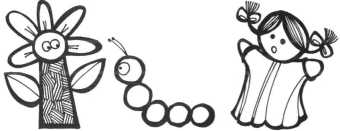

- **be manipulated,** and, better yet, constructed as a reward for children who have shown definite signs of catching the "reading bug." The "Build a Bookworm" page that follows is intended for such use.

BUILD A BOOKWORM

MATERIALS NEEDED

- 5 connected yarn balls (Deco Pom or Pom Decor)
- 2 medium sized skewer sticks or narrow doweling about six inches long
- 2 small eyes (wiggle eyes, sequins, felt, or beads)
- bits of yarn, felt, pipe cleaners, etc.,for feelers, tail, horns, spines, or legs
- white craft glue
- scissors

DIRECTIONS

1. **Glue a stick to each of the end pompons.** The best way to do this is to part the "fur" of the pompon and squirt a drop of glue down inside. Then poke the pointed end of the stick into the pompon where you put the glue, and pinch the "fur" back around the stick. Twisting the stick as you poke it in will help hold it in place. When you have attached both sticks, lay your puppet aside so that the glue can dry.

2. **Think about what kind of character you want to make,** and what materials you will use for things like eyes, feet, and feelers. How about a caterpillar with spots of colored felt? A miniature dragon with paper wings and pipe-cleaner feet? A worm with tiny button eyes? Assemble the things that you will need.

3. **When the glue holding the sticks in place is dry,** you may decorate your puppet. Move the eyes around to decide what kind of an expression you want your puppet to have. Then glue them to one of the two ends of the row of pompons. Add feet, horns, spots, or whatever you decide looks best to make the puppet character you want.

FLOPPY EARS RABBIT

POP-UP SOCK PUPPET

Floppy is a rabbit **hand puppet** that can be made from household materials in a matter of a few minutes. With a little adult assistance and supervision, children can make their own rabbit puppet characters from discarded socks.

Through expressive head, nose, and ear movements, Floppy does a lot of talking, pantomimed or voiced. He can pop up, look in any direction, jump or hop around, then suddenly disappear down a hole. His extra long ears can react to sounds or show feelings by perking up, "scissoring," clapping together, or flopping over. With a nose that really twitches, he can sniff out curious situations. The versatility of this rabbit puppet is pointed out by the following suggested uses.

As a commentator . . . Floppy can respond to sounds heard while trying to sleep in his hole by leaving messages, popping up and moving around, or talking with a puppet voice. He can show excitement about upcoming events, discontent about the lack of politeness, encourage the use of better voice control, or even help teach vowel sounds.

As a pet rabbit . . . Floppy can help children become better informed about proper pet care, or prepare children for visiting and handling different kinds of animals.

As a magician's rabbit . . . Floppy can pop out of a hat and tell children some magic tricks and what it's like to live with a magician. (The "Hector the Director" puppet from Chapter Four would make a good magician.)

To promote literature appreciation and motivate reading . . . Floppy can relate personal experiences from contacts with famous rabbit characters, like the Easter Bunny or Beatrix Potter's *Peter Rabbit*. He could interview a Bugs Bunny puppet.

Floppy can direct children or be used by them to act out the following poetic verse:

Here is a bunny
   with ears so funny,
And here is a hole
   in the ground.

Each sound that he hears,
   He pricks up his ears
And pops in the hole
   in the ground.

As a science teacher . . . Floppy can comment on the weather, pretending to notice drops of water running into his hole. He can sniff the air and wonder why it doesn't smell as fresh as it used to. He can tell about his life in the forest, and what he and his animal friends experienced during a fire.

To encourage creative writing . . . Floppy can ask children to write letters to him while he is out busily helping the Easter Bunny. Older children can be asked, and will generally enjoy writing the responses for Floppy. (See letter-writing form on pages 71 and 72 of this chapter.)

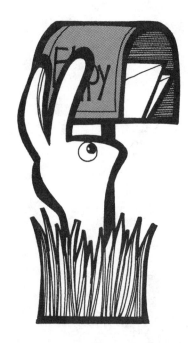

As a musical director . . . Floppy can be used by a child or adult to lead rhythmical group movement to the "Bunny Hop." If each child has his own puppet, the puppets can hop in unison, moving in a line, tilting their heads in place of leg movements.

MAKING A FLOPPY EARS POP-UP RABBIT

MATERIALS NEEDED

FOR THE RABBIT'S BODY

Fuzzy, textured socks are nice. Large quantities can often be found in laundromat lost and found boxes, or may be purchased inexpensively at thrift shops or rummage sales.

FOR THE RABBIT HOLE

A cylinder in the form of an oatmeal box, dull-edged tin can, or section of wide cardboard tubing is needed. It should be large enough for the rabbit on the puppeteer's hand to pass through easily.

FOR THE GRASS

Green crepe paper or felt works well. A piece big enough to wrap around the cylinder with a little overlap and extend about three inches or nine centimeters beyond the length of the "hole" is needed.

FOR THE RABBIT'S FEATURES

The *whiskers* can be made from pipe cleaners, fine telephone wire, or stiffened string, thread or yarn. Any of these would poke out on either side of a cloth or button nose. A *mouth line* can be stitched in or drawn on a light-colored sock with a permanent ink marking pen. The *eyes* can be made from ordinary buttons or the craft store movable ones can be stitched or glued into place.

FOR COMPLETING THE RABBIT CHARACTER

Cotton balls can be added for cheeks, paws, or a tail. Odds and ends can be added as desired for completing the rabbit character and his costume. For example, a necktie would look nice on a magician's rabbit.

FOR CONSTRUCTING THE PUPPET AND HIS HOLE

A sewing machine is handy, though a needle and thread are adequate for stitching up the ears. Other items needed are scissors, thick craft glue, cellophane tape and masking tape.

DIRECTIONS FOR ASSEMBLING FLOPPY AND HIS HOLE

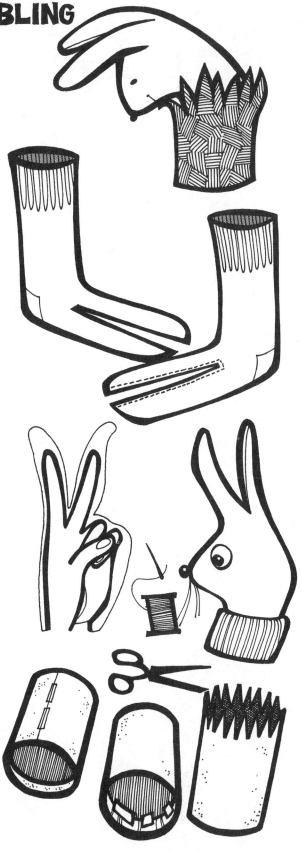

1. Decide which side of the sock is best for the rabbit's body. Make sure this good side is on the inside of the sock when you do the sewing.

2. Snip down from the center of the toe through *both* thicknesses of sock, stopping a little ways above the heel. If the toe has a hole, or if shorter ears are desired, cut the ears accordingly.

3. Using a sewing machine or needle and thread, stitch up the "V" to form the rabbit's ears. Check to make sure the stitching is holding well all the way around, then turn the sock inside out.

4. Put the puppet on, noticing the hand positions illustrated in this chapter. Practice moving the ears and nose, as this makes it easier to decide where to locate the features. Go ahead and add the features to the rabbit's head by gluing, stitching, marking or poking. Add other details such as a costume now or when glue is dry.

5. While the glue is drying, make Floppy's hole. Attach the grass so that about one inch or three centimeters of material is left over at the bottom edge of the cylinder. Attach crepe paper with cellophane tape, *not* with glue. Felt can be glued or stitched into place. Finish the bottom edge by folding the excess grass material up into the rabbit's hole. Use masking tape to hold it in place. Cut the excess material at the top of the hole to look like grass.

_____ ___,19___

Dear Floppy,

_____

_____

_____

_____

_____

Love,

_____

_____ _____, 19____

Dear _____,

_____

_____

_____

_____

_____

Love,
Floppy

FLOWER FANTASY
EXPRESSIVE GLOVE PUPPET

An advantage of the flower glove puppet is that it can be carefully manipulated by the operator, showing development and use of refined and sensitive control of hand and finger movement. This type of action is an effective means for communicating to viewers who are at fairly close range. Useful in both performance and instructional situations, the flower glove puppet can be made from an ordinary glove.

CONSTRUCTING THE FLOWER PUPPET

THE GLOVE

Obtain gloves from rummage sales or thrift stores, or by requesting children to bring them from home. Gloves can also be made from yardage scraps, in which case a pattern can be made by tracing around the hand and arm of the puppeteer, leaving plenty of margin. Gloves which go further down the arm are easier to use because additional "stem" material may then not be needed.

THE STEM AND LEAVES

The leaves can be made out of crepe paper, felt, or other material—or simply cut off of artificial flowers. "Streamer" leaves made of a scarf-type fabric add a nice effect if the puppet will be twisting.

Practice manipulating the flower puppet *before* attaching the leaves so as to determine the best placement. Use needle and thread or heavy-duty craft glue, connecting the leaves so that they move freely as the puppet is operated.

THE FLOWER

Flower designs will vary, depending not only upon the type of flower, but the character—realistic or fanciful. One flower could have a center complete with stamens and pistils, whereas another might have a face in the middle.

If the growth of a plant is to be shown, be sure to make the petals of a size that can be concealed fairly well when the hand makes a fist. Snaps or velcro might be used if petals or seeds are to drop off the puppet.

THE FLOWER POT

A flower pot can be made from wide cardboard tubing, a coffee can, an oatmeal box, etc. A plastic or cardboard pot will work, and can generally be found at a dime store or nursery.

ALTERNATE FLOWER CONSTRUCTION METHOD

A different, simpler type of pop-up flower can be made using a dowel rod for the stem and a styrofoam ball for a base on which to build the flower. Petals, leaves, etc. can be added as needed to complete the character.

STAGING YOUR FLOWER FANTASY

ROOM 4 PRESENTS
Flower Power

For a simple performance a flower pot stage can be operated out in the open, behind a table, or using a hand puppet stage. (Refer to Appendix B for examples of easily constructed stages.)

If a number of children are to participate at one time, a garden or hillside setting might be more suitable. Use a mural for a backdrop. A large, open space stage such as this provides lots of room for movement of puppets and puppeteers.

DRAMATIZING FOR MOVEMENT AND LANGUAGE EXPRESSION

1. Move the flower puppets rhythmically and to the mood of music, using controlled arm, wrist, hand and finger action.

   a. Puppeteer partners can take turns mirroring each other's puppets.

   b. Once effective movements are established, a performance can be developed with solo and group routines. This could be incorporated into a longer show including other types of puppets.

2. Let the puppet express feelings through its movement—reaching, drooping, etc.

   a. Use the puppet to reflect the situation at hand, or the mood of a story.

   b. Develop a pantomime where passers-by do or don't notice beauty or fragrance. Children or other puppets (rabbit, bee, etc.) could play the parts of passers-by.

3. Develop a simple plot with interaction between a flower or flowers and other puppets. For example, a rabbit might be digging a hole too close to the roots, or a caterpillar could be munching the plant's leaves.

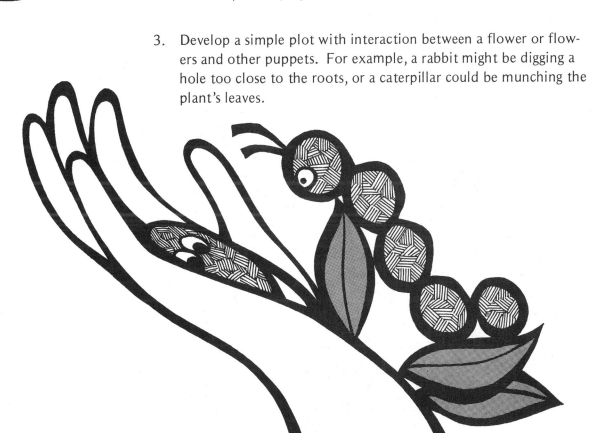

DRAMATIZING FOR SCIENCE CONCEPT BUILDING

1. Show the stages of plant growth: seed, stem and leaves, then bud and flower.

2. Show plant growth in relationship to what plants need in order to grow. Use stick puppet sun, raindrops, and other props and sound effects where appropriate.

   a. To demonstrate a plant's need for water, let the flower wilt when thirsty, then make "drinking" sounds and straighten up as it is being watered.

   b. Have the puppet lose a few seeds to imitate seed dispersal as it dries up. This action can be combined with movement created by wind blowing, thereby creating a good opportunity to help teach the rebirth factor in the life cycle of a plant.

   c. Pollination can be demonstrated through the use of several flower puppets and simple stick puppet bees.

3. THE PLANT EXPERIMENT

Hector the Director or *King Canine,* characters from Chapters Four and Six, can conduct plant experiments, asking children to follow directions with actual plants or puppet flowers. For example, some plants could be ordered removed from light exposure, while others are told to stay. *Hector* or *King Canine* could ask children to hypothesize what will happen after one week.

Hector could play the role of The Mad Scientist, inventing silly experiments, making mistakes, using incorrect reasoning, and much more—all of which would be corrected by children and flower puppets. This, obviously, is an excellent way to reinforce learning without resorting to routine methods for reviewing important concepts.

4. THE FLOWER SHOW

Here is an opportunity to combine science, art, and drama into one performing experience for a group of children.

Each child turns his glove into a particular species of flower, showing appropriate colors, petal patterns and leaf shapes. The setting might be a flower show, a garden, or a hiking trail, depending on the types of flowers used. The flower puppets could be introduced by a judge, a gardener, or a backpacker. As introduced, each puppet could tell (or even brag) about its unique characteristics: color, shape, smell, and use to insects or humans.

A judge might ask a flower, "How did you get so beautiful?" The flower would naturally have to thank the sun, the water, the soil, the bees, and the air for their teamwork in making it beautiful. In a similar fashion, a gardener could explain that it takes a variety of flower types—tall and short, single and double—to make his garden look beautiful. A hiker might stop at each flower on his trail, interview it, and discover how each is adapted to its environment. What part does each one play in Mother Nature's plan? Does it provide nectar for hummingbirds? Do its roots prevent erosion? Are its leaves food for caterpillars?

FLOWER SHOW

Any of these approaches could end with flowers being picked. For example, the hiker might try to pick one as he ends his last interview. Puppet flowers readily "wilt" when pulled off the puppeteer's hand by a human actor or hand puppet. This action could be used to emphasize reasons for not picking flowers:

1. They would no longer be there for the enjoyment of other passers-by, including animals such as birds and insects which may depend upon them.

2. Some flowers, such as many wildflowers, should never be picked, as they are on endangered species lists and are protected by law. They will become even more scarce if not given a chance to reproduce according to nature's plan.

LISA AND THE SONGBIRD
A COMPLETE PUPPET SHOW PRODUCTION

To introduce children to the ingredients and mechanics of puppet theater, this chapter offers suggestions on how to involve a group in a simple yet complete puppet production. The experience lays groundwork for possible future performances.

The hand puppet girl and string puppet bird provide an opportunity for experiencing two different puppet types in one play. This mixture is quite commonly used by professional puppeteers. Today's audiences also see performances where the puppeteers are in full or partial view, and this arrangement also occurs in the production of Lisa and the Songbird.

Marionettes are often avoided because they are thought of as being too complicated to construct and manipulate. There are, however, a number of simple approaches to making string puppets, such as the two methods shown in this chapter for the bird marionette. Likewise, the stage, scenery and props for *Lisa and the Songbird* are presented in simplified construction steps. These easy though effective puppetry techniques offer a starting point for children who, after having experienced this complete production, are likely to initiate and build their *own* puppet shows.

PREPARING TO INTRODUCE THE PLAY

1. **Read through the script** for *Lisa and the Songbird* found on pages 81, 82, and 83 of this chapter.

2. **Collect the materials** needed and follow the directions provided for making the two puppets, the scenery, and the bird cage.

3. **Locate the other items** needed for the production:

   Spotlight: A goose-neck lamp, large flashlight, shielded light bulb, or some type of projector will suffice.

   Instruments: Other types can be substituted for those suggested at the beginning of the script. For example, student-made musical instruments or even pots and pans can be used to create different kinds of sound effects.

   Small Table or Bench: A child's desk or a piano bench is used as a base upon which to stand up the scenery, and together these two items create a simple stage.

   Piece of Cloth: A sheet, bedspread, tablecloth, or large towel is draped over the bench or table in the stage building process.

   Box: A sturdy cardboard box is needed in order to introduce the play *Lisa and the Songbird* according to the presentation method described in this chapter. It should be large enough to hold all of the production items mentioned above, minus the table or bench, of course. It can be reinforced and attractively decorated.

4. **Make one or more copies of the three script pages** for *Lisa and the Songbird*. A copy should be placed in the box with the other materials needed for this puppet play.

LISA AND THE SONGBIRD

A narrator reads the script while puppeteers manipulate the characters. If possible, musical instruments should be used to accompany the actions of each of the characters.

LISA — xylophone or tone bells
SONGBIRD — flute or slide whistle
SONGBIRD while flying — music box or jingle bells
FLOWERY CAGE — bells or tambourine
COZY COTTAGE — triangle or drum

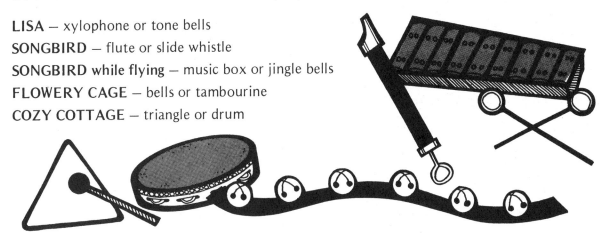

Once upon a time there was a girl named LISA who lived all alone in a COZY COTTAGE. She worked hard to keep her home tidy, but there were many times when she would just sit by the window and sigh. "I'm so lonely," she would say. "I wish I had a friend out here in the country." Finally, one day after she had sighed her umpteenth sigh, the COZY COTTAGE said, "Look out my window, LISA. See how happy the robins and blue jays and woodpeckers are? Maybe you should find a bird to be your friend."

"That's a wonderful idea!" she cried, and she almost flew out the door of her COZY COTTAGE. Later she returned from the pet shop with a FLOWERY CAGE and a beautiful SONGBIRD inside. "I'm so glad I picked you, SONG-BIRD," LISA said. "You'll be my friend forever in our COZY COTTAGE." On hearing his good fortune, SONGBIRD hopped around in his FLOWERY CAGE and sang a cheerful melody for LISA.

He sang so sweetly that LISA opened the FLOWERY CAGE and danced across the room while SONGBIRD flew once around the COZY COTTAGE, twice around his FLOWERY CAGE, and three times around LISA because he loved her best of all. Then, instead of returning to his FLOWERY CAGE, SONGBIRD landed right on top of LISA's head! "Oh, SONGBIRD, you are so much fun, and you make me so happy. But it is getting late, and you must go back inside your FLOWERY CAGE." LISA carried him on her head over to his FLOWERY CAGE, and with a happy chirp, SONGBIRD hopped back to his perch.

Outside, the moon shone brightly down on the COZY COTTAGE. LISA yawned and said, "I'm so sleepy. SONGBIRD, won't you please sing me to sleep?" SONGBIRD perked up his weary head and sang LISA the softest lullaby she'd ever heard. The moment she climbed into bed, LISA fell fast asleep.

The next morning SONGBIRD awoke before LISA. To his surprise, the door to his FLOWERY CAGE was still open! He was so happy that he hopped off his perch, flew once around the COZY COTTAGE, twice around his FLOWERY CAGE, and three times around LISA because he loved her best of all. Again he landed right on LISA's head.

Just as LISA awoke, SONGBIRD heard the sound of a distant rooster, and he flew out the open window of the COZY COTTAGE. Rubbing her eyes, LISA said, "What was that?" She went over to the FLOWERY CAGE and wailed, "Oh SONGBIRD, where are you? Please come back to your home. We love you." But SONGBIRD was nowhere in sight. LISA was very sad as she looked up at the empty FLOWERY CAGE. "Oh COZY COTTAGE, why did you leave your window open?"

That evening LISA called again from the window of the COZY COTTAGE. "SONGBIRD, we miss you. Please return. Who will sing me to sleep?" But SONGBIRD did not return. LISA sighed as she went over to the FLOWERY CAGE. She made sure its door was wide open and inside there was plenty of food and water. Then she lay down on her bed in the COZY COTTAGE. "Ahhhh choooo!" she sneezed from the cold air coming through the open window. "Where will SONGBIRD stay on such a cold night?" she wondered. Without his soft lullaby, she had a hard time getting to sleep.

The next morning LISA awoke with a start and rushed to the FLOWERY CAGE. Alas, SONGBIRD had not returned. All day long she sobbed and she sighed. Then, just at sunset, LISA heard a faint, familiar melody. "Could that be SONGBIRD?" she said as she clasped her hands. And sure enough, it was, and all of a sudden SONGBIRD was flying once around the COZY COTTAGE. LISA danced with happiness as SONGBIRD flew twice around his FLOWERY CAGE and three times around LISA whom he loved best of all. Instead of landing on LISA's head, SONGBIRD went straight to his FLOWERY CAGE and quickly gulped all his water and ate all his food. And just as quickly, he fell fast asleep on his perch.

"SONGBIRD," asked LISA, "why did you leave us? Aren't you happy here?" But SONGBIRD was too tired to answer. "Shhhh. He sleeps," the COZY COTTAGE called out in a whisper. "SONGBIRD," LISA persisted, "what made you leave our happy home?"

"Shhhh! Can't you see he's back to stay," the COZY COTTAGE scolded. "He flew around once because he missed me and twice because he missed his FLOWERY CAGE. And for you he flew three times because he missed you most of all. SONGBIRDS get lonely, too, if no one can hear their sweet melodies."

With SONGBIRD back on his perch at last, LISA went right to sleep dreaming of happiness to come. The FLOWERY CAGE heaved a happy sigh, and the COZY COTTAGE quietly closed its shutters.

—— THE END ——

INTRODUCING LISA AND THE SONGBIRD

Appearing throughout this section of the chapter are **dialogue sections** which are presented as a guide for an adult who is preparing to introduce *Lisa and the Songbird* to a group of children. It is assumed that, in addition to providing an entertaining show, the purpose of this puppet play experience is to teach a group of youngsters how to go about planning and performing a complete puppet production. Puppet theater terminology should be carefully used and presented throughout this introductory process. Of course the level of expectation and teaching style will depend on the nature of the group.

PUPPET SHOW INGREDIENTS
STORY   LIGHTING
SCRIPT   SPECIAL
NARRATOR   EFFECTS
CHARACTERS   MUSIC
PPETEERS   DIRECTOR
AGE   PRODUCER
ENERY   STAGE MANAGER
ROPS   AUDIENCE

"We're going to perform a puppet show! There are many things needed in order to prepare and perform a puppet play, so in this box I put some items that I figured would come in handy. I picked out these items by first thinking about the important ingredients that are necessary for putting on any puppet production."

"What do you suppose I mean when I say puppet show ingredients? (Accept responses.) That's right, the particular things that belong together in order to make something complete—like the cooking ingredients that are mixed together to make a cake. You certainly wouldn't want to leave the flour out when following a cake recipe, and we wouldn't want to leave out an important ingredient when preparing a puppet production, either!"

"So . . . right now, let's think about and figure out what the ingredients are for building and performing a puppet show. We need to have a list of these things before deciding how each of us will actually participate in our puppet production. Raise your hand when you're ready to suggest a puppet show ingredient. If you happen to mention an ingredient that ties into an item I brought for our puppet production, I'll reach into this box and bring it out for all of us to see."

Take suggestions in random order until all of the essential puppet production ingredients have been mentioned and briefly discussed. Throughout this introductory process, help children to learn puppet theater vocabulary by repeatedly using the theater terms that are defined on the following four pages. They are presented using words appropriate for young children, and descriptions are given to show how the terms relate to performing *Lisa and the Songbird*.

Involving youngsters in puppet production experiences while they are hearing and using theater terminology is the best way to help them learn the full meaning of these new words. To assist them with remembering and reading the terms, and to help organize the teaching process, make picture-word cards or record information on a chalkboard or chart as the ingredients for a puppet show are suggested or studied.

CHARACTERS
The characters are the actors in the play. You can tell who or what the characters are by reading the script.

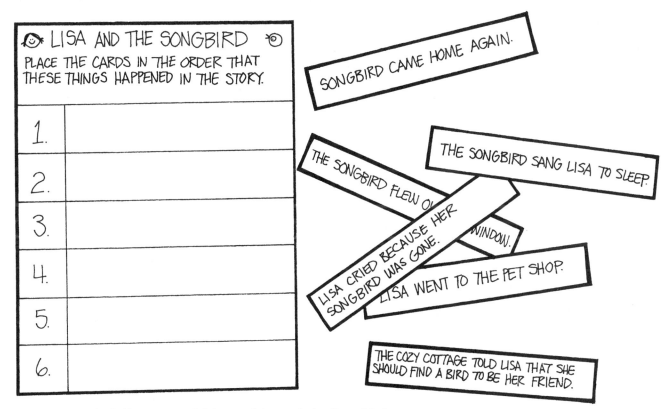

Provide follow-up activities to *Lisa and the Songbird* that include constructing, writing, drawing, sequencing or guessing-game experiences. In this way, important ideas can be reviewed and reinforced.

THEATER TERMS FOR LISA AND THE SONGBIRD

STORY

A story is a series of events that are tied together by a main idea called a theme. A complete story should have three main ingredients: characters, action, and a setting. A story plot is developed by having beginning, middle, and ending sections. **Let's look for these elements as we dramatize LISA AND THE SONGBIRD.**

"That evening, Lisa called again from the window of the cozy cottage..."

SCRIPT

A script tells the story, using dialogue and stage directions. **The script for LISA AND THE SONGBIRD is written on these three pages.**

NARRATOR

A narrator is a person or puppet that introduces the story and tells it to the audience. **In our play there is a human narrator who reads all the parts and uses a different voice for each character.**

CHARACTERS

The characters are the actors in the play. You can tell who or what the characters are by looking at the script. **In our puppet play there are two puppet characters plus the parts played by the flowery cage and the cozy cottage.**

PUPPETEERS

Puppeteers are the people who operate or manipulate the puppets (but they often carry out other theater jobs which include light technician, stage manager, narrator, director, and producer). **How many puppeteers do we need for our play? (Two.) In LISA AND THE SONGBIRD, a narrator will read the script, so our puppeteers will not speak the voices for the puppets. Instead, they will concentrate on manipulating the puppets, and will control the puppet action with careful hand, finger, and arm movements that are appropriate for each puppet character.**

STAGE

A stage is the performance spot for the puppet action. Some puppet stages have elaborate scenery, built-in lighting, and several curtains. Others, like ours, are much easier to build. We'll use this table (put it into position) and this cloth (pull it out of the box and drape it over the table) to build our stage for LISA AND THE SONGBIRD.

SCENERY

Scenery is composed of a backdrop and props that are used to create a setting, or an environment, which usually suggests the time and place of the story to the audience. **Our scenery forms the top part of our stage, and will create an opening through which our audience will watch the puppet action in our play.**

PROPS

Props are any items besides the puppets that are used on the stage platform during the performance. **The bird cage is an important prop in our play, and adds to the scenery to help create the setting. It completes the set and is placed on the apron or performing platform of our stage, which is created by the flat top surface of the table.**

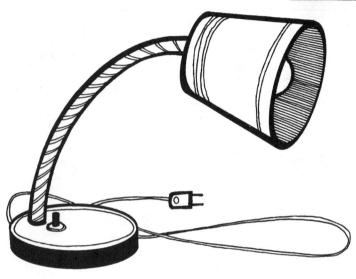

LIGHTING

Lighting includes all that is done with lights to create a theater setting, set a mood, and give the audience a clear view of the show. Light technicians are part of the stage crew. In addition to operating the stage lights used during a performance, they must also operate the house lights which are usually turned off during a performance. **For LISA AND THE SONGBIRD we will need this spot light. (Take it out of the box.) How many light technicians do you think we will need for our production?**

SPECIAL EFFECTS

Special effects are used during a show to create an illusion or draw special attention to something. Special effects are often created with lights, music, or magical tricks. **In our production instruments will be played just as each character's name is mentioned by the narrator. For LISA we will use a xylophone (get it out of the box, and do likewise for the remainder of this sequence.) For the SONGBIRD, we'll use a slide whistle. When the bird flies around, the audience will hear a tune coming from this music box. The sound of this tambourine will stand for the FLOWERY CAGE, and the COZY COTTAGE's sound effect will be this small drum.**

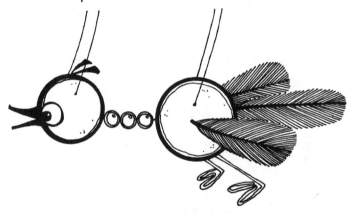

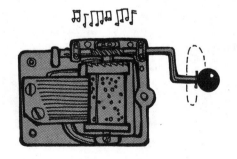

MUSIC

Music is often used to create a mood. Songs and their lyrics are sometimes part of the dialogue. **During our show, musical instruments will be played to create sound effects and will add some background music during the narration of the story.**

DIRECTOR

The director is the person who tells the performers how to speak or sing their lines and how and where to move. The director might ask for more voice projection or better enunciation. **In our play the director will also be the prompter, giving the performers and stage crew cues to let them know just when to do things. During a performance, the director is usually back stage or off-stage. For our play however, the director is also the narrator, and must stand next to the stage in view of the audience.**

PRODUCER

The producer acts as a supervisor, making suggestions and giving directions while overseeing all aspects of the entire performance project.

STAGE MANAGER

The stage manager is the person responsible for the use and good working order of the whole set: props, scenery, and lighting.

AUDIENCE

Those who watch a performance are members of the audience. Sometimes people are invited by special invitation, while at other times they purchase tickets in advance or upon entering the place where the performance is to occur, which may be a theater or an auditorium. What does an audience do to show appreciation for a performance?

Depending upon the time element and the children, it might be advisable to stop at this point and continue the play introduction at another session. In between sessions children could think about and even try out some of the "ingredients"—puppets, spot light, instruments, script.

"Now that we're aware of all the important ingredients needed for our puppet production, let's prepare for the performance. Since I have practiced how to say the lines in the script and am prepared to give directions to the performers and the stage crew, I will be the narrator, stage manager, director, and producer!"

At this point use a planned strategy for selecting puppeteers, light technicians and instrumentalists. Give each child a chance to ask questions and briefly practice as a means of rehearsing for the first performance. Give manipulation tips to the puppeteers and show them how to position their bodies in relation to the stage, as pictured on the first page of this chapter.

Though special effects "technicians" are generally not in view of the audience, the instrumentalists should sit in a row facing the stage so that they can both watch the puppeteers and receive cues from the narrator-director. Ask or tell the children about the ways an audience is important to a play production. Use this as an opportunity to reinforce how good, cooperative behavior makes the performance a more enjoyable experience for everyone involved.

When children feel fairly secure about what to do and where to be, walk a few steps away from the stage area. Make eye contact with the performers and the stage crew to let them know that the show is about to begin. Then signal the light technicians to turn off the house lights and focus the spotlight, letting the audience know that the show is starting. As introducer, walk over to the front of the puppet stage and announce,

"Ladies and gentlemen, welcome to our Puppet Show, LISA AND THE SONGBIRD. It is presented for your enjoyment by (insert name of group)."

Step aside and begin narrating and directing. Instrumentalists will be so intent on watching the puppets that they will probably need individual cues to play immediately as character names are stated in the narration.

During the last line of the play, slowly move the cozy cottage backdrop, circling it around until the back side is in front of the puppets. This action will clearly indicate to the audience that the performance has now ended. Following the applause, ask the participants in the production—puppeteers, instrumentalists, and light technicians—to come forward one at a time as they are introduced. Ask them to remain and form a line in front of the stage, then help them to bow properly as a group. Give the light technicians their final cue. **"House lights, on. Spotlight, off."**

It might be desirable to repeat the puppet play with a new group of performers and technicians from amongst the audience. When the performing is finished, and before excusing the group, pack up the box. Use the packing process as an opportunity to review some of the theater terms that were introduced during the production experience.

Following their participation in *Lisa and the Songbird,* children will undoubtedly want to perform more puppet shows. Though individual children will voluntarily do puppetry on their own, additional types of puppetry experiences should be planned and introduced. There are many suggestions for simple skits in this book and in the references listed in Appendix E. Furthermore, the programs and materials already familiar to the group or the adult leader generally provide a good source for puppetry experiences.

Puppet construction is a good follow-up activity to *Lisa and the Songbird.* However, before deciding to involve a group in a puppet making experience, answers to the following practical questions should be considered:

- What puppet construction materials are readily available as household "junk" or as items which could be purchased inexpensively in large enough quantities?

- Should a construction method be introduced if it requires the purchase of materials?

- How much time is needed for making a particular kind of puppet? Would several work sessions be involved?

- What kind of puppet construction will fit into the time that is available for puppet construction?

- Is advance preparation required by adults or group members prior to beginning the construction?

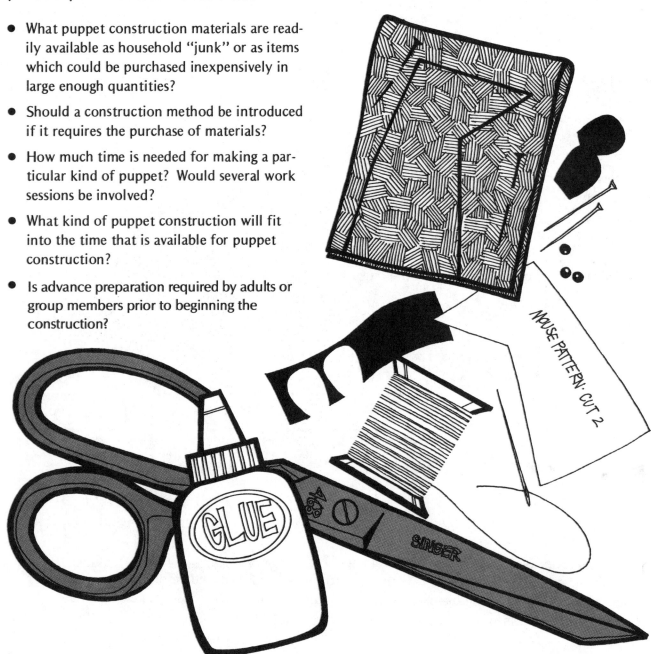

Keeping in mind the answers to the above questions on cost and availability of materials, time blocks, and preparation requirements, an adult should then give careful thought as to what approach might be used when introducing puppet construction to children:

How will the children be organized for using the puppets?

- Will they work in small groups to prepare productions or simple skits based on something like folktales?

- Will they work individually or with partners on different components needed for one complete set of materials for a large group production such as could be done with a story like *Lisa and the Songbird*?

- Will each child work alone to make his puppet? If so . . .

  — Will this puppet be used for improvisation, such as through the use of an interview technique like the one described with "Interview Starters" in Chapter Two?

  — Will it become part of a pre-planned large group production, such as would be the case when performing as a "wild thing" in the story *Where the Wild Things Are*?

  — Will the child perform alone with the puppet, such as through the use of a "mouse house technique" described in Chapter Seven, or as a community helper telling about the work it does?

☺☺ PUPPET PARTNERS ☺☺
FOR THE FINGER PUPPET FESTIVAL MAY 12

THE 3 LITTLE PIGS   Monica Martin
                     Elizabeth Booth
JACK AND THE BEANSTALK   Jeff Wilson
                        Becky Rogers
LITTLE RED RIDING HOOD   Chris Carson
                        Brad Farnsworth
THE THREE BEARS   Laura Baker
                  Michael Davis
CINDERELLA   Linda Hamilton
             Maria Sanchez
THE PIED PIPER   Scott Kelly
                 Dick Travis
THE UGLY DUCKLING   Erin Gray
                    Judy Nickerson
THREE BILLY GOATS GRUFF   Rick Fisher
                          Juan Jimenez
PUSS IN BOOTS   Dan Dewey
                Rod Branson
RAPUNZEL   Andy Alderson
           Erica Hamilton
SLEEPING BEAUTY   Kim Christianson
                  Alan West

How will the puppet construction be presented?

. ∴ as a basic construction technique which can be used to build a variety of characters, such as the egg carton method shown in Chapter Two or the sock puppet variety illustrated in Chapter Six?

. . . as the creation of a character that will be used in one or more suggested or pre-planned ways, such as the caterpillar in Chapter Eight or the flower in Chapter Ten?

. . . as an independent project in an activity center where the construction is a reward for following printed directions which may or may not include specific uses for the puppet, such as can be developed for the "Jack in the Box" character in Chapter Three or the witch mask of Chapter Five?

☝ PUPPET OF THE MONTH ☝
Let's make Lisa!

To make this puppet, you will need:
- a styrofoam ball
- a square piece of cloth
- two rubber bands
- yarn or fur for the hair
- buttons or beads for the eyes
- scissors
- glue

Lisa is a hand puppet.

This is how to put your hand inside.

DIRECTIONS
1. Make a face on the styrofoam ball, which is the puppet's head.
2. Glue on some fur or yarn for hair.
3. Choose a piece of cloth for your puppet's body. Put the cloth on your hand and then put on the head and rubber bands.

CLOTH SQUARES

⊗ BUTTON BOX ⊗

Yarn

GLUE   GLUE

STYROFOAM BALLS

RUBBER BANDS ☆

Of course, any puppet built for a specific use can also be used—and, indeed, *will* be used— on an improvisational basis. **By creatively using a combination of the teaching strategies presented in this chapter an adult can be reassured that children have been helped to grasp concepts that can be applied on a broad basis—not only to all forms of theater production, but to the problem solving and pleasure seeking of every day's new adventures in living.**

"LISA" SIMPLE HAND PUPPET

This is an easy-to-make puppet that can rapidly change its costume—or even its head! The body is simply a cloth square draped over the puppeteer's hand and attached to the thumb and forefinger with rubber bands or curtain rings. The head is a styrofoam ball with a hole carved out to fit the puppeteer's forefinger.

You can make interchangeable heads with different expressions for one character,

or a whole set of different characters!

Look in the "Hector the Director" chapter for instructions and ideas for making puppet heads from styrofoam balls.

HOLD HAND IN POSITION

DRAPE WITH CLOTH, PUT RUBBER BANDS ON THUMB AND FINGER

ADD STYROFOAM HEAD

ADD ACCESSORIES

Your "costume department" can simply be an assortment of 12"–18" cloth squares, in various prints, colors, and fabrics. Flannel can be used to indicate pajamas, bandanas are great for cowboy puppets, and silk scarves add mood and movement to ghosts and dancers. Other simple accessories, such as necklaces, shawls, and corsages, may be draped, tied, or pinned to the costume after it is on the puppeteer's hand.

Children operating Lisa in the play will enjoy selecting her outfits from the costume department.

SONGBIRD MARIONETTE
MATERIALS AND EQUIPMENT NEEDED

Two styrofoam balls or egg shapes, one about 1½" diameter, the other about 2½" diameter.

Black carpet thread   White glue

3 or more pipe cleaners   Masking tape

Narrow strips of wood (molding works well): two 4" pieces and one 7" piece; felt scraps, beads, sequins, etc. for features and trim.

3" string of plastic beads (these beads, fused to a connecting string, are sold in decorator shops and drapery departments.)

5 or 6 large, brightly colored feathers

Hammer   Small nails   Scissors   Ruler   Straight pins

CONSTRUCTING THE MARIONETTE

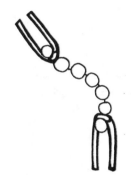

1. The beads form the neck which connects the styrofoam head and body. To attach the neck, you will first need to cut two 3" lengths of pipe cleaner. Twist each pipe cleaner around one end of the bead chain as shown, going 1½ times around and bending the pipe cleaner ends so that they extend beyond the end of the beads.

2. Poke the pipe cleaners into the styrofoam head and body. Your puppet should now look like this:

3. Now you can give your bird its wings and tail. Carefully poke feathers into the styrofoam.

4. You can make a beak for your puppet by cutting out a diamond-shaped piece of felt, using this pattern. Fold the beak in half and pin it to the head.

Make eyes for the bird from felt, beads, sequins, or whatever you have. Use straight pins to fasten them to the head.

5. Bend pipe cleaners to form your puppet's legs and feet, and poke them into the underside of the body.

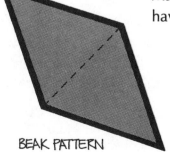

BEAK PATTERN

STRINGING THE MARIONETTE

1. First, build the control by carefully gluing and nailing the two 4" crosspieces one inch from either end of the 7" piece of wood.

2. Next, taking into consideration the position you will be in when operating the puppet (sitting, kneeling, standing) and the type of stage to be used (tabletop or on the floor), decide how long you want the strings to be. Then cut 4 pieces of carpet thread, adding 3" to the desired length to allow for attaching to the puppet and control.

3. Cut four 2" pieces of pipe cleaner and bend them like this ✌. They will be used like staples to attach the strings to the puppet. Gently poke the pipe cleaners into the styrofoam, one on either side of the head and one on either side of the body (towards the top and back a little). In each case leave a small loop of pipe cleaner sticking out, and tie one of the threads to each loop. Then push the pipe cleaners all the way in.

4. Ask someone to hold your marionette for you, with the bird about as far below the control as you want it to be when the strings are attached. Then take one body string and attach it to the end of one of the rear crosspieces, winding it twice around the stick and securing it with tape. Next, attach the other body string in the same way, making sure that the body hangs straight.

WRAP STRING AROUND CONTROL   SECURE WITH TAPE

5. Attach the head strings to the front crosspiece. If you ever need to untangle the strings of your marionette or change their length, all you need to do is remove the tape and make the desired adjustments.

6. You can manipulate your puppet by tilting the control from front to back or side to side.

WALKING BIRD MARIONETTE
MATERIALS AND EQUIPMENT NEEDED

Two styrofoam balls or egg shapes, one about 1½" diameter, the other about 2½" diameter.

Six 3" lengths of pipe cleaner   Two metal washers, about ¾"-1" diameter

Two 6" lengths of thick yarn   Black carpet thread

Narrow strips of wood (molding works well): one 6" piece and one 4" piece

3" string of plastic beads (these beads, fused to a connecting string, are sold in decorator shops and drapery departments.)   Masking tape

Felt scraps for making beak and feet   White glue

5 or 6 large, brightly colored feathers   Straight pins

Beads, sequins, etc. for features and trim   Hammer and small nails

Tracing paper   Pencil   Ruler   Large needle

CONSTRUCTING THE MARIONETTE

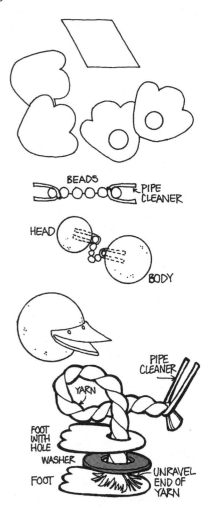

1. Trace the foot and beak patterns, and transfer them to scraps of felt. You will need one beak shape and four foot shapes. Cut these shapes out. In two of the foot shapes, cut holes as indicated by the circle on the pattern. Set the feet and beak aside for now.

2. The beads form the neck which connects the styrofoam head and body. To attach the beads to the styrofoam, wrap a separate pipe cleaner piece 1½ times around each end of the bead chain, as shown, then press the ends of the pipe cleaner pieces into the head and body shapes.

3. Use two straight pins to attach the felt beak to the head.

4. The two pieces of yarn form the legs. Bend a pipe cleaner piece around one end of each leg, as you did with the neck. Slide a felt foot piece with a hole onto the other end of each leg. Then add the metal washers, which give the feet weight and make them easier to control. Pull apart and spread out the end of the yarn piece. Spread glue onto the bottom foot pieces (without holes) and glue each pair of foot pieces together with the washer and yarn in between.

5. Attach the legs to the body by inserting the ends of the pipe cleaners into the styrofoam. Be sure that the feet face forward.

6. Poke feathers into the body shape to form the tail and wings. Make eyes of felt, beads, sequins, etc. and attach them with straight pins.

STRINGING THE MARIONETTE

First, build the control by joining the two strips of wood at right angles as shown, using small nails or tacks.

Cut two 16" lengths of carpet thread, one 10" length, and one 8" length. Use a needle to attach one 16" thread to each foot, making a big stitch and tying it. Bend the two remaining pipe cleaner pieces into shapes and tie one of the shorter threads to each one, as shown. Poke the pipe cleaner with the 10" thread into the body about ⅔ of the way back; poke the pipe cleaner with the shorter string into the top of the head. String placement may be adjusted later for balance.

Attach first the body string, then the head string, then the leg strings to the control as shown, using strips of masking tape. This type of control is called an "airplane" control.

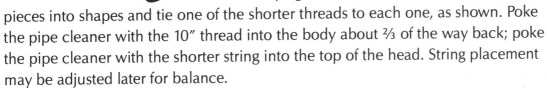

MANIPULATION

Tilt the "wings" of the control to make the puppet walk. Move the head and body by tipping or twisting the "body" of the control. Can you make your puppet dance? Walk up or down stairs? Take a bow? Stamp its foot? Walk backwards?

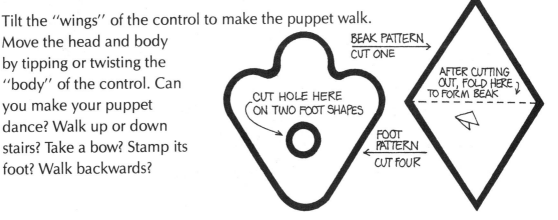

BEAK PATTERN
CUT ONE

AFTER CUTTING OUT, FOLD HERE TO FORM BEAK

CUT HOLE HERE ON TWO FOOT SHAPES

FOOT PATTERN
CUT FOUR

THE COZY COTTAGE

The Cottage is made from two pieces of heavy cardboard hinged with cloth tape. You may "paper" the cottage with wallpaper, contact paper, or construction paper. Cut a window and tape acetate or cellophane over it. "Furniture" is simply flat cloth or paper shapes. Cottage folds flat for storage.

THE FLOWERY CAGE

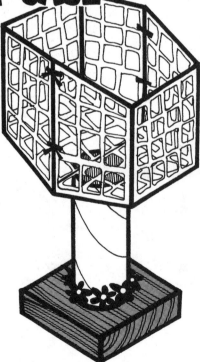

To make the cage, you will need:

2 plastic berry baskets
A cardboard tube
A block of wood about
   1" × 4" × 4"
White glue
Masking tape
Wire "twisters" (used for closing
   plastic bags)
Small artificial flowers
Scissors/paper punch

1. Glue and/or tape the tube to the block of wood. Set this base aside to dry.

2. Cut one side from each of the baskets. Then use twisters to fasten the baskets together, with the open sides at the top of the cage.

3. Punch holes on opposite sides of the top of the cardboard tube, and put a twister through each hole. Use these twisters to attach the cage to the base.

4. Decorate the cage with artificial flowers. You may wish to cover the tube with paper.

I KNOW AN OLD LADY
SHADOW PUPPET PLAY

There is magic in a shadow. It invites imagination and suggests character through shape and movement. It is no wonder that shadow puppetry has intrigued mankind for hundreds of years. It continues to be performed not only in the Far East where it is believed to have originated, but all over the world in both traditional and exciting new forms.

Before undertaking the shadow puppet play *I Know an Old Lady*, the following general information about shadow puppet construction and performance should be examined.

SHADOW PUPPET MATERIALS AND CONSTRUCTION METHODS

Ancient and traditional forms of shadow puppets are carved from parchment or animal skin. Usually these have intricate designs, requiring numerous jointed parts, several rods, and master puppeteers. The shadow puppet techniques described in this chapter, however, use readily available materials. The performance methods suggested are suitable for beginning puppeteers.

BODY

FRINGE

NET →

LEAVES BETWEEN WAX PAPER

Simple yet amazingly effective shadow puppets can be constructed with household "junk" items such as tissue paper and yardage scraps, cardboard, and aluminum foil. Non-opaque materials such as colored cellophane, gauze, or even cut glass forms provide many opportunities for experimentation. Acetate, clear plastic meat trays, or lids from take-out soft drinks can be cut to shape and marked with some types of felt-tipped pens.

A variety of flat-shaped objects can be ironed between two pieces of wax paper, stuck onto clear contact paper, mounted on a sheet of clear acetate, or used just as they are! Odds and ends, such as fringe, netting, or lace can be added to create a textured look and extra movement. Eyes and other details can be cut or punched out for character development. Interesting effects will result by placing colored cellophane or dangling objects in these cut out parts.

It might be easiest to begin experimenting with body designs by tearing or cutting out shapes from something as inexpensive and available as newspaper. After determining the shape and making sure any jointed parts will overlap, transfer the puppet pattern to heavy paper or lightweight cardboard. This can later be strengthened by adding clear contact paper to one or both sides, if necessary. For young children, use dark material throughout the body-design process. This makes it easier for them to imagine shadow outlines, which requires distinguishing silhouettes from ordinary drawings.

Beyond adding fringe or dangling objects, creating jointed parts offers exciting and more advanced ways for shadow puppet movement. This movement could very well be important to character development or to the action within a play. For example, it is important that the Old Lady have a jointed jaw in order to carry out the major action of swallowing in *I Know an Old Lady*.

Once the desired movement is established, experimenting should occur to determine which puppet parts should move and which should remain stationary. Deciding precisely where the parts should be hinged is the next step, though this can be altered after the puppet is completed. The parts should overlap at the points where they will be loosely joined. A hinge can be formed by knotting carpet thread on either side of needle-poked holes. Paper fasteners (brads) also make satisfactory hinges, and are especially easy for young children to use. They should be placed through punched-out holes and opened in a way that permits free movement of the puppet parts.

JOINTS

SIDE VIEW OF THREAD JOINT

PAPER FASTENER THROUGH PRE-PUNCHED HOLES

Any of the following can be used for shadow puppet rods: bicycle spokes, strong steel wire, dowels, skewer sticks, straws, or ribs from old umbrellas, which already have holes in them for easy connecting. The rods should not be held rigidly against the puppet's body, as this would limit the puppeteer's operation of the puppet. Rather, they should be loosely attached with loops of thread or fine wire and positioned to allow for the best possible movement of the puppet. The end of a rod might already have a hole, or with some materials a hole can easily be made. If not, however, there are several ways to fix rods in order to attach them to puppets:

RODS

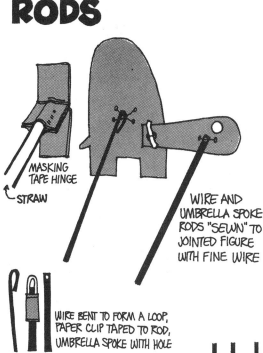

MASKING TAPE HINGE

STRAW

WIRE AND UMBRELLA SPOKE RODS "SEWN" TO JOINTED FIGURE WITH FINE WIRE

WIRE BENT TO FORM A LOOP, PAPER CLIP TAPED TO ROD, UMBRELLA SPOKE WITH HOLE

1. If it is a wire rod, it may be possible to bend the end around to form a small, closed loop.

2. Affix a paper clip so that a small part of it extends beyond the rod.

3. Use masking tape around the end of the rod and onto the puppet itself, forming a flexible hinge.

No matter what type of rod is used, it is wise to tape a piece of polyfoam or cloth around the exposed end for protection and added control of the puppet. A wide piece of dowel can be drilled and slipped over the end of the rod, or a large wooden bead will sometimes be just the right size for making a handle.

POLYFOAM · BEAD · DOWEL HANDLES

SCENERY

SCENERY HUNG FROM ABOVE

POCKET OF CARDBOARD BELOW SCREEN TO HOLD SCENERY

SCENERY ON RODS FITTED INTO A BLOCK OF WOOD

Scenery is easily made from lightweight cardboard. The construction methods mentioned in the above sections on bodies, joints, and rods also apply to the making of scenery. For example, colored cellophane can be affixed behind window openings. A mat knife can be very handy in cutting out small areas, such as between branches of trees.

The most common way to use scenery in a shadow play is to place it directly on the screen where the puppets are operated. Large pieces can be attached with tape, clips, or velcro. Small scenery items at the bottom of the screen can be held in place with rods: to the back side of the scenery tape a long rod that extends down below the screen and fits into one of a series of holes drilled into a woodblock, or pokes into a long strip of styrofoam or polyfoam. (More information on scenery is presented on page 105 in the section titled **Light Sources**.)

STAGES

If the shadow puppets are no taller than ten to twelve inches, a stage with a shadow screen of about 2½ x 4 feet is a good size. Sometimes a picture frame of about the right size can be located. In some instances a frame is needed that fits specially into a hand puppet stage. A simple stage can be designed by starting with a piece of plywood, masonite, or heavy cardboard box and cutting out an opening of a desired size and shape.

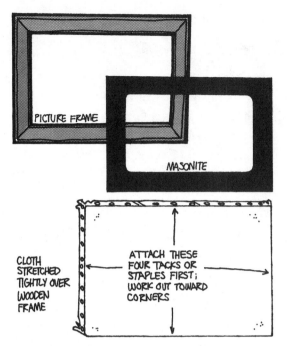

PICTURE FRAME

MASONITE

The white screen material can be a type of paper or cloth, and should be attached as wrinkle-free as possible into the frame. Cloth can be dampened before the stretching process so that it will have an extra-tight fit when dry.

CLOTH STRETCHED TIGHTLY OVER WOODEN FRAME

ATTACH THESE FOUR TACKS OR STAPLES FIRST; WORK OUT TOWARD CORNERS

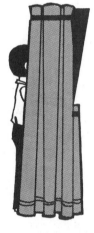

The shadow puppet stage opening should be positioned high enough so that the puppeteers can either sit or stand below it as they operate the puppets. Generally, the screen part of the stage is tipped at a slight angle downward towards the audience. This makes the puppets more visible to the audience and helps in controlling the puppet movement. Of course, in working with young children, a simple stage might not have, nor would it necessarily need, the tilted screen.

It is usually desirable to have some way to block off excess light and backstage activity from the audience. Though curtains may be hung on a wooden framework specially built to contain the shadow screen, other arrangements can be made when using a self-supporting shadow screen that is raised up by its own structural base or is secured to a covered bench or table top:

- If performing where there are draw curtains, as on an auditorium stage, bring the curtains up to the edge of the shadow screen.

- Place the shadow screen in a door opening or entrance way.

- on either side of the screen place tables on end, movable chart or coat racks, or accordion screens, draping with cloth or decorating as needed.

THE MAGIC SHADOW THEATRE

THEATRE BUILT TO FIT IN A DOORWAY

LIGHT SOURCES

SHEET WITH OPAQUE CURTAIN
BELOW, TIED BETWEEN 2 POLES

LIGHTS SET UP
BACKSTAGE

For some very informal shadow work on a bright day, the sun is a perfect light source! Generally, however, one or two lamps of 100 to 150 watts should be placed about 4 to 6 feet behind the screen, focused downward, and in such a way as to diffuse the light as evenly as possible over the screen. There should be no shadows from the puppeteers themselves if the light is correctly positioned.

OVERHEAD
PROJECTOR

PUPPET WORKED
DIRECTLY ON THE
PLATFORM

TRANSPARENCY WITH
SCENERY

A handy light source available in most schools and many libraries is an overhead projector. With its use comes a range of exciting alternatives:

ACETATE SHEET WITH WAVES PULLED ACROSS
PLATFORM WHILE PUPPET SURFS

MICE DRAWN ON ACETATE SHEET;
FLEXIBLE TAILS MANIPULATED BY RODS

1. An entire scene can be projected onto the shadow puppet screen through the use of a colored or black-and-white transparency. Original designs drawn onto clear plastic with colored marking pens or ink can be projected. In fact, the acetate can be re-used if water soluble pens are used. Transparencies can also be made by several types of copy machines and come ready-prepared in some educational materials kits.

2. A long strip of plastic depicting an on-going scene can be pulled slowly across the platform to give the illusion of a puppet on the shadow stage traveling while only moving in place. A transparency could even be jiggled to create an earthquake effect.

3. Small scale puppets can be operated directly on the projector platform, in which case an entire show can be projected from the overhead projector onto a shadow screen. Some of the small figures could be drawn onto a large acetate sheet, though could still have moving parts with rods.

2 PROJECTORS
FOCUSED ON THE
SAME SCREEN

4. A more involved technique allows for smooth, quick scene changes and interesting special effects by using two overhead projectors focused at one time on the same screen. Several people work together with blockout devices and carefully organized performance materials.

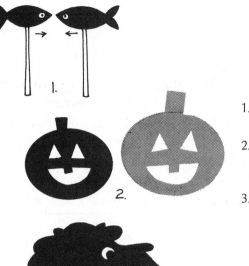

SHADOWS CAN BE TRICKY

1. For shadow puppet movement to occur in the opposite direction, a duplicate puppet facing the other way is needed.

2. Shadow puppets are generally operated against the screen. However, as a special effect, the puppet can be moved back from the screen to increase its size and make its silhouette less defined.

3. Disappearing acts and magical transformations can be done convincingly and quite easily. Small shadows can be absorbed into larger ones to create this illusion. For example, as the Old Lady swallows the fly in the shadow production described below, the fly's shadow merges with the Old Lady's to create the swallowing effect.

DRAMATIZING "I KNOW AN OLD LADY"

Children nearly always enjoy dramatizing familiar stories in new ways. The lengthy character sequence for this play can be practiced by unscrambling cards which have the characters' names on them. If the familiar tune that is often associated with *I Know an Old Lady* is sung, the audience can be invited to participate in the singing, and this can add to the fun of the production.

There are plenty of jobs to keep everyone busy: manipulating puppets, operating lights, leading singing (could use word cards and microphone), designing the set, stage managing, directing, and even producing the play. (Please refer to pages 86 and 89 of Chapter Eleven for further information on production roles, procedures, and theater terminology.)

The simplified puppet show instructions on pages 86 and 89 should serve as a guide for preparing to introduce *I Know an Old Lady*. They are intended for use by children on an independent basis following, or in place of, the group's experience with this production. An independent activity center can be created by bringing together the following items: sample puppets, puppet patterns, script, instruction sheets, and materials for making individual puppet show sets.

Room 18 Proudly Presents
I KNOW AN OLD LADY
PRODUCED AND DIRECTED BY MRS. SIMPSON
Puppeteers: Kim Crisman, Tami Adams, and Scott Sanford
Light Technicians: Brad Williams and Chuck Carlson
Set Design: Pam Boyd, Ann Wilson, Lisa Wells, and April Avilar
Stage Manager: Amy Anderson
M.C.s: Rick Rogers and Doug Taylor
Ticket Sales: Beth Bradley
Ushers: Jim Booth, Bill Vanier, Mike Fay
Chorus: Janet Aster, Melanie Benson, Becky Carlson, Meg Davis, Linda Evert, Monica Fields, Anita Garcia, Bob Hill, Kent Ingalls, Kevin Little, Michael Martin, Sandy Nickerson

Poster by April Avilar

I KNOW AN OLD LADY*

1. I know an old lady who swallowed a fly;
    I don't know why she swallowed a fly,
       I guess she'll die!

2. I know an old lady who swallowed a spider
    That wriggled and wriggled and tickled inside her;
    She swallowed the spider to catch the fly,
    But I don't know why she swallowed the fly,
       I guess she'll die!

3. I know an old lady who swallowed a bird,
    Now how absurd to swallow a bird!
    She swallowed the bird to catch the spider
    That wriggled and wriggled and tickled inside her.
    She swallowed the spider to catch the fly,
    But I don't know why she swallowed the fly,
       I guess she'll die!

4. I know an old lady who swallowed a cat,
    Now fancy that, to swallow a cat!
    She swallowed the cat to catch the bird, . . .
       . . . [Repeat previous parts to make
          each verse progressively longer.]

5. I know an old lady who swallowed a dog,
    My what a hog, to swallow a dog!
    She swallowed the dog to catch the cat, . . .

6. I know an old lady who swallowed a goat,
    Just opened her throat, and in walked the goat!
    She swallowed the goat to catch the dog, . . .

7. I know an old lady who swallowed a cow,
    I don't know how she swallowed a cow!
    She swallowed the cow to catch the goat, . . .

8. I know an old lady who swallowed a horse.
    That killed her of course!

Puppets for Dreaming and Scheming
© 1988—The Learning Works, Inc.

107

* I KNOW AN OLD LADY (WHO SWALLOWED A FLY)
Words by: Rose Bonne   Music by: Alan Mills
Copyright 1952 by PEER INTERNATIONAL (Canada) Ltd.
© Copyright 1960 by PEER INTERNATIONAL (Canada) Ltd.
Sole Selling Agent PEER INTERNATIONAL CORPORATION
Used by Permission

THE OLD LADY WHO SWALLOWED A FLY
A SHADOW PUPPET SHOW

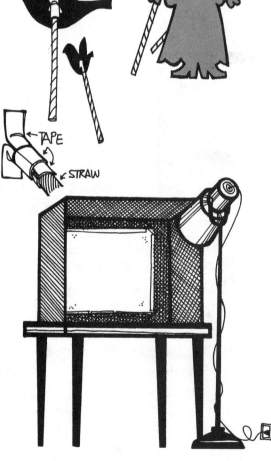

THE STORY

- What happens in the story?
- Learn what is first, second, third, and so on.
- Practice singing or saying the story until you know it by heart.

1. Old lady alone on stage
2. Fly buzzes in and old lady swallows it
3. Spider comes hopping along and jumps into mouth
4. Bird flies into mouth
5. Cat comes in slowly, lady bends over, eats it
6. Dog hurries in barking, jumps into mouth
7. Goat prances in, gets eaten
8. Cow ambles in, is eaten with great effort
9. Horse comes trotting along, is swallowed with even greater effort, whinnies faintly
10. Old lady dies!

THE PUPPETS

- Cut apart the animal shapes on the dotted lines that are on the three puppet pattern sheets.
- Trim carefully around each puppet shape.
- In order to work the puppets, they need handles or rods. Attach one plastic straw to the back of each puppet with masking tape. The Old Lady will need two rods. She is the only puppet that is jointed.

ROD HINGE DETAIL
ATTACH TAPE TO SIDE OF PUPPET
←TAPE
←STRAW

THE STAGE

- Make your own stage from a cardboard box.
- Cut out a large opening.
- Put white paper or cloth across the opening to make a shadow screen.
- Put a light up high and a few feet away from the back side of your stage. Point it down to light up the shadow screen.
- There may be a stage that is set up for you or your group to use.

THE SHOW

IF YOU ARE GOING TO PERFORM BY YOURSELF . . .

- Put the puppets in the order that you will need them.
- Say or sing the story as you work the puppets.
- You might ask a friend to tell or narrate the story while you work the puppets.

IF YOU ARE GOING TO PERFORM WITH OTHERS . . .

Decide WHO will do WHAT:

- work each puppet
- sing or narrate the story
- work the lights
- direct the show

- invite the audience
- introduce the show
- introduce the puppeteers
- thank the audience for coming

Presenting
THE OLD LADY WHO SWALLOWED A FLY

Practice three or four times as a group before you invite an audience. Watch each other perform, and, in a nice way, give helpful hints to make the show better.

NOW WHAT? MORE SKITS!

- Keep your puppets in a bag or box that has your name on it.

- Tell what is inside by writing on the outside of the bag or box.

- Next time you get out your puppets, you may want to try a new puppet skit. Here are a few ideas, but you will have ideas of your own, too. Remember to move the puppets to words or sounds as you perform the skits.

1. Have the dog and cat be friends, get into a chase, and then be friends again.

2. Have the Old Lady complain about the fly that is buzzing all around her.

3. Have the fly tease the spider and then get caught in the web. To do this, drape a web across the shadow screen. Make it from paper, yarn, netting, pipe cleaners, or wire.

4. Make a nest for the bird to sit in. Let the bird explain what it is like to have baby birds hatch.

5. Have an animal talent show. Each puppet can sing, dance, tell a joke or ask a riddle. The Old Lady or the audience can decide who wins the talent show.

6. Have the horse and cow talk about the farm they live on. They can explain how they help the farmer make a living.

ATTACH ONE ROD TO BODY AND ONE TO JAW.

HINGE 2 PIECES AT DOTS, USING A PAPER FASTENER

THE OLD LADY

JAW

SHADOW PUPPET PATTERNS

SPIDER

BIRD

FLY

CAT

DOG

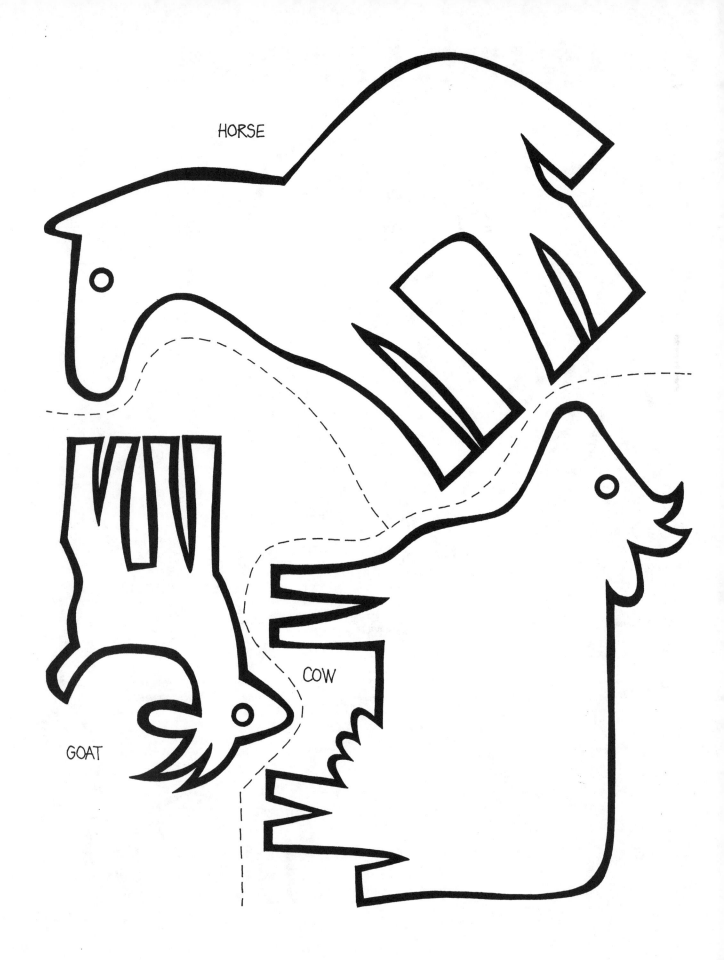

HORSE

COW

GOAT

BEHIND·THE·SCENE TIPS FOR BEGINNERS IN PUPPETRY

I. BUILDING A SHOW
PREPARING THE GROUP

Before organized production becomes a group project, it is best for new puppeteers to experience improvised acting and simple skits, such as through the interview session and situation story techniques mentioned in Appendix C and Chapters One, Two, Three and Twelve.

The adult directed puppet shows within this book are good examples of ways to introduce performance techniques and theater terminology (see Chapter Eleven). The puppet manipulation pointers and performance guidelines listed later in this appendix section can be included in preliminary work with puppets as appropriate, so that when the group plans its own show, individuals will have learned some performance standards and will have a good background for all facets of building a show.

SELECTING THE CONTENT

Skits acted out on an informal basis often contain themes and spark new ideas which can be developed into good show material. Several short acts can be put together to form a complete production which can be performed on one or several stages. Familiar stories such as those listed in Appendix E can also provide a good starting point for puppet shows.

An increasing number of puppet play scripts can be found within children's books and puppetry books, including many of the books listed in Appendix E. The Puppetry Store, also noted in Appendix E, sells some separate scripts as well as books which contain a collection of scripts.

Here is a list of topics from which content for puppet programs can emerge:

      words, proverbs, jokes, riddles
      television shows, quiz games, vaudeville, sports events
      famous people, historical events, impersonations
      works of art, pictures, songs, dances, musical numbers
      dreams, common problems, daily life routines or predicaments
      poems, nursery rhymes, fairy tales, fables, folktales

No matter what subject is used, there should be plenty of action in the skit. The story line should be complete, introducing, developing and resolving conflict.

GETTING READY TO CONSTRUCT

Before starting to make a puppet or build scenery and props, it is helpful to be familiar with a full range of possible construction materials. This generally insures that the result will be original and intriguing puppets and sets. Have a place for collecting and organizing the following types of odds and ends into containers or on shelves:

- old bottle brushes, scouring balls, steel wool mops, fly swatters, wooden and plastic spoons and hair curlers

- broom handles, dowels, popsicle and other wooden sticks, coat hangers, umbrella parts, bicycle spokes, and chop sticks

- plastic containers, small boxes including egg cartons, plastic and wooden baskets and trays, used rubber balls, ping-pong balls, and tennis balls

- buttons, beads, sequins, glitter, costume jewelry, bits of glass

- corks, sponges, lids and caps, spoons and spools, weights and fishing floats

- socks, stockings, gloves and mittens, felt and other cloth scraps, polyfoam, cotton, kapok and other materials to use for stuffing

- lace, fringe, pom-poms, trimmings, netting, feathers, fur bits, embroidery thread, raffia, ribbon, shoe laces, string, yarn and rope

- pipe cleaners, chenille, wire, tooth picks, and tinsel

- styrofoam balls, sheets and packaging shapes, wood scraps, sponges and old leather goods or scraps

- old dolls (especially rag dolls), doll clothes, doll house furnishings, hats, wigs, and stuffed toys

- colored construction paper, crepe paper, molded and corrugated paper and cardboard from packaging, sheets of different weight cardboard, shiny, fuzzy, or transparent flat materials (wallpaper sample books are a good source), cellophane, metallic paper, paper plates, bags and cups, cardboard and plastic tubes, old newspapers and magazines

- natural objects and materials such as unspun wool, gourds, shells, pebbles, seeds, seed pods, twigs, etc.

In addition to an "odds and ends center," it is a good idea to organize a separate **equipment center**. In a group situation, make sure that everyone is familiar with the contents and correct use of staplers, paper punches, masking and cellophane tape, scissors, etc., *before* construction begins.

Help the group to realize and discover the many different ways in which objects can be attached or connected with paper clips, brads, staples, stickers, glue, tape, tooth picks, pipe cleaners, needle and thread. In some instances materials can be joined together simply by poking, folding, bending, hooking, or twisting.

Other equipment and materials which should be organized separately from "odds and ends" include rulers, pins, tacks, marking pens, crayons, paints and brushes, liquid starch, water cans, and scissors. In addition, a hammer, nails, wire cutters, pliers, saw, and sand paper will be necessary for some types of projects. By providing many options for making puppets and other show materials, individuals will learn a range of construction techniques. Puppetry tends to promote this, as it is an art which combines many skills.

Comparisons of puppets is inevitable during the construction period. This is fine as long as it is emphasized that each person's puppet is a unique creation of individual expression. Throughout this phase give reminders about returning equipment and picking up work areas, and *be sure* to allow time to involve the group in clean-up at the end.

Many approaches to puppet construction and building simple sets are illustrated within chapters of this book. The following portion of Appendix A supplements this material.

MAKING THE PUPPETS
PUPPET HEADS

More than any other part of the puppet, the head must express *personality*. This should be done in a simple way, as details are often lost, going unnoticed and unappreciated by an audience. In most instances, it is best to keep an expression quite neutral and to let the voice and movements of the puppet show the emotions. The size of a human puppet's head should be no smaller than one-sixth the length of the body.

The following methods and materials are some ways to approach puppet head construction:

- STYROFOAM ball or egg shape: can be shaped by adding things and cutting away sections, using a heated awl; eye sockets can simply be poked in.

- PAPIER-MÂCHÉ: can build this over crinkled-up newspaper, styrofoam, or balloon.

- SOCK: can be used almost as is for many puppets; can be stuffed and decorated, or pulled over a puppet head shape such as a ball or plastic bottle.

- SPONGE: can be used as it is or can be shaped with scissors.

- POLYFOAM: half-inch or three-quarter-inch sheets can be cut and formed into any shape; contact cement is best, though heavy-duty craft glue is recommended for young children.

- CLOTH: felt, muslin, and fake fur are among the types most frequently used.

Some instant and "junk" puppet heads can be made by using one of the following as a base: vegetables or fruit, paper plates, cups, spoons, fly swatters, blocks of wood, boxes, gourds, paddles, balls, plastic containers, and such.

It is important to consider how the head will be attached to the puppet's body, unless a stick already comes down from the head material, such as with a fly swatter. In some cases a rod or finger hole can be poked into the head. In other instances, such as for hand puppets, a cardboard tube should be attached. A tube or stick might need some felt cloth added in order to have a surface on which to attach the costume. The tube should fit so as to permit good control of the puppet's head.

FACIAL EXPRESSIONS AND FEATURES

As mentioned above, puppets are more effective with simple, clearly defined and exaggerated features. The sizing and position of the features is pertinent to character development, as shown by the following illustrations:

FEATURE BOARD

A feature board with movable parts offers a fun and helpful guide for deciding just how to get the kind of look that is intended. Experimenting with differently shaped and colored eyes and noses is particularly valuable as a beginning experience. Changeable mouths, ears, eyebrows, moustaches, beards, and wigs can be included and could be used in conjunction with a variety of shaped heads. Styrofoam shapes, such as wig stands, could have features simply pinned on. A flannel board for use with some felt and velcro backed shapes is another approach.

HAIR

Hair in the form of wigs, beards, moustaches or eyebrows can be pinned, taped, glued, stapled, or stitched onto a head, depending on the head and hair materials. Narrow streamers of crepe paper, shredded plastic bags, strips of curled shaped ribbon or construction paper, scrub pads and steel wool, fur pieces, unspun wool, wood shavings, feathers, string, and yarn can be made into wigs, depending on the effect that is desired.

EYES

Give the puppet's eyes sparkle! Use a touch of glitter, the head of a pin or tack, a sequin or a shiny button on the puppet's pupils, perhaps making this the light spots in the eyes.

For quickly made eyes, use various colors and sizes of stick-ons, which are generally available at stationery or office supply stores. Several stick-ons can be used together. A black, felt-tipped permanent ink marker can be used to make a dot for the pupil.

For some characters, loosely attached movable eyes will be effective. Buttons and ping-pong balls can be stitched on in such a way that they will move as the puppet moves. Hobby and craft stores sell manufactured movable eyes where the pupil moves freely. Some puppetry books show mechanized ways to achieve sideways or up and down motions of eyeballs.

HANDS OR PAWS

Above all, these should be exaggerated! Felt is frequently used, in which case the hand should be stitched and *then* cut out. Stuffing may include some fine wire. Here are some simple hand designs:

COSTUMES AND BODIES

As pointed out in this book, a puppet can be a musical instrument, a tooth, or even a hammer! The simplest of hand puppets uses a handkerchief for a costume. A basic hand puppet costume can be used with interchangeable heads and removable clothing items. (See Chapter Four.) A shirt, or a sleeve off a shirt can be a good base for a costume. Sometimes doll or baby clothes fill a need.

Here are some important points about puppet costumes, most of which relate to hand, rod, or stick puppets:

- Make the costume long enough to extend to the end of the operator's forearm.

- Use a material that hangs well when the puppet is motionless and moves easily with the gestures of the puppeteer's hands *without* restricting mobility.

- For skirts to flow, leave them unhemmed, if possible; this is particularly important if the puppet is to dance.

- For a hand puppet, the costume will last longer if an outer costume is built on top of an inner body costume.

- Select a texture and color that suits the character; it may be a good idea to check how the cloth looks under the stage lights.

To make the most of each puppet, draw upon a collection of hats, coats, vests, sashes, scarves, bandannas, aprons, glasses and changeable features that can be quite easily added and removed, perhaps even during a performance, and where appropriate, in view of an audience. Small props such as baskets or umbrellas can be kept in a box with such items as those mentioned above.

CONSTRUCTING SCENERY

Scenery not only makes a production more attractive, it helps set the time and place of the action. It can be as simple as a single flower, or as complex as a jungle. Generally it is best to use only what is needed to suggest a setting, and to let the audience imagine the details. Elaborate scenery has a tendency to detract from the puppets and can interfere with a smooth production.

Often a solid colored backdrop is all that is needed. Puppeteers operating hand or rod puppets frequently use a piece of cloth called a *scrim*. This hides them, but through it they can watch the action on stage. Scenery pieces are placed around the stage opening, hung from poles, or affixed to the backdrop with pins or velcro. They can be made from cardboard, plywood, or built from odds and ends.

Small scenery pieces can be attached to a rod and held in place with a puppeteer's free hand, the use of a clamp, or a slotted holding device. If built with a base, a scenery piece can be wedged firmly in between two stationary panels of wood that are attached to or are part of the stage. An advantage to this type of scenery is that the puppets can act all around it, and it can quickly be changed in full view of the audience. Some ideas for scenery pieces include trees, bushes, flowers, fences, cars, boats, beds, waves, houses, tables, chairs, wagons, or even bathtubs!

A backdrop with a scene drawn or painted on it is well suited to plays where quick scene changes are not required. The setting might depict an underwater environment, a village street, a country road, a castle, cave, jungle, cottage or even outer space. The scene should not appear cluttered, and objects should be clearly defined.

Made on heavy paper, a window shade, a starched sheet or other type of cloth, a backdrop can be tacked onto a wall or back panel, draped from a rod across the back of the stage, or poked through a slot in the stage. Quick scene changes can occur when using the rear projection method on a translucent backdrop.

USING PROPS

The things that a puppet uses during a performance—handbag, box, table, ball, or cup—are called properties or props. A slotted playboard can help to hold these items in place, or other holding devices such as those mentioned above under "scenery" can be used.

Most types of hand puppets can pick up, carry, and set down a variety of objects. For rod or stick puppets, attach the object to a thin, stiff wire or wooden rod and move it as the puppet is moved. In some instances, it may work to attach the prop directly to the puppet using velcro, wire, pipecleaners, a paperclip, snap, rubber band or string.

Items frequently used as props include hammers, knives, flags, guns, swords, pies, umbrellas, fishing poles, brooms, handkerchieves, hats, tooth brushes, hand fans, and baskets. Doll house furnishings and toys or things made from boxes, cups, wire, etc. also can make good props.

An entire skit can be built around a single puppet or prop. For example, perhaps using only pantomime, a character could come across a lovely flower, smell it, react in several ways, and finally decide to pick it.

PLANNING THE LIGHTING

Darkening a room and illuminating the puppets with spot lights or stage lights not only helps an audience to see the show, but builds a theatrical atmosphere by providing a focal point for the viewer's attention. Experiment with lighting up the acting area in different ways and from varied angles above, below, in front, behind, and to the sides of the stage opening. Examine the shadow patterns as some lights are turned on while others remain off.

If a scrim curtain is used, artificial lighting will be necessary to hide the performers. Special lighting effects and moods can be created with the use of black lights, colored cellophane, dimmer switches, flickering lights, back-lit scenery, lit-up props, rear-view projection, and so on.

Many types of readily available lights and fixtures are suitable for puppet shows. A quick and easy method is to beam light directly onto the performing area from a slide, filmstrip or overhead projector. Goose-neck or draftsman's lamps, sockets with clamps, or lightbars are quieter and offer an additional range of lighting options. **If lights are to be specifically purchased, 50 to 100 watt P.A.R.** spot or flood lights work well and are relatively inexpensive.

Back stage lights may be necessary when performing in a darkened room, in which case commercially made night lights will suffice. It is important that the backs of all lights be covered to keep them from shining in the eyes of the audience. Bulb housing can be easily made using tin cans, such as coffee cans, which can be spray painted black. Make sure all light cords are placed where no one will trip over them. Where possible, attach them overhead, or at least tape them down.

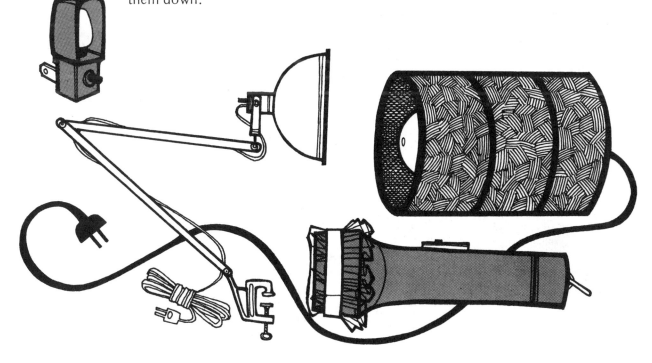

INCORPORATING MUSIC AND SOUND

Music can add variety and excitement to a puppet show in numerous ways. It can be used just before the show to let the audience know that the play is about to begin, during scene changes, at the conclusion, while the audience is exiting, as background to puppet action, in direct relation to puppet action, and for special mood and other effects. Music can be live—singing, humming, playing of an instrument, improvised sounds—or recorded.

Here are a few of many musical selections that can be used in ways mentioned above:

Brahms — waltzes
Debussy — Golliwogs
Herbert — March of the Toys
Haydn — Surprise Symphony, Toy Symphony
Mozart — Serenade in G
Prokofiev — Peter and the Wolf
Ravel — Mother Goose Suite, Bolero
Rimsky-Korsakov — Flight of the Bumble Bee, Scheherezade
Saint-Saens — Carnival of the Animals
Stravinsky — Firebird Suite, Petrouchka
Tchaikovsky — Nutcracker Suite, Sleeping Beauty, 1812 Overture
Wilson — Seventy-Six Trombones

For particularly scary themes, try one of the following:

Dukas — Sorcerer's Apprentice
Grieg — The Hall of the Mountain King, March of the Dwarfs
Liszt — Mephisto Waltz
Mussorgsky — A Night on Bald Mountain
Prokofiev — Cinderella Suite
Saint-Saens — Danse Macabre

For a fairly complete listing of music for different situations, look in *Marionettes Onstage* by Leonard Suib and Muriel Broadman.

Musical sounds and sound effects make a puppet production more lively and vivid. Unusual and comical sounds can result from the use of bells, drums, gongs, cymbals, castanets, triangles, whistles (including slide whistles), horns, rattles, natural objects such as gourds or coconut shells, and even pots and pans.

SPECIAL EFFECTS FOR SOUNDS AND ACTIONS

thunder	Bend a heavy sheet of cardboard or a piece of tin violently back and forth so that it moves in waves.
rain	Sprinkle dried peas or rice onto a metal baking dish, or roll marbles around in a cardboard carton.
wind	Use human sound effects, or pull a smooth stick across a tightly stretched piece of silky material.
galloping horses	Alternately and rhythmically tap two small wooden blocks or strike upsidedown cups on a wooden floor or board.
gurgling stream or boiling liquid	Put a straw into a cup of water and blow hard.
mist, fog, or smoke	Blow corn starch or baking soda through a narrow tube by squeezing a container filled with this which is attached to one end. Dry ice can be sprinkled with water just prior to the time for the special effect. A fire extinguisher can be let off for a few seconds at a time.
waves in the ocean, a lake, or a river	Painted muslin or silky material can be held at either end and moved.
fire	Create dancing shadows in front of a red light by placing something that moves in front. Streamers can be placed on the front side of a fan at low speed.
flash of light, as for lightning	Use a flash attachment from a camera; flick stage lights on and off quickly.
wilting flower	Make stem using curtain spring; insert rod, then, when wilting is to take place, pull rod out a ways.
snow or magic dust	Throw up soap flakes or paper confetti.
balloons and party blowers	Affix balloon or blower to mouth of puppet with a hidden plastic hose that extends to the puppeteer's mouth. This method can be adapted for other clever uses, e.g. balloon can be used to show chest breathing in and out, or stomach getting larger and larger.

Puppeteers often enjoy inventing ways to make special effects that are required or suggested by scripts or story lines. Sound effects records are available, however, and can come in very handy for certain effects. A tape recorder can be used to record needed sounds, such as street noises, sawing noises, or animal sounds.

II. PREPARING TO PERFORM
A. GIVING A PUPPET LIFE

Two things should happen when a puppet is created: (1) it should have a distinct personality; (2) it should move in ways that convey emotions. It is a combination of facial expression, costume, movement, and voice that create a puppet's uniqueness. Character development will come forth during the construction, but will be expanded through improvisation as the puppeteer practices manipulating the puppet. (See sections A and B under "Building A Show" at the beginning of Appendix A.)

VOICE

After learning how to operate a puppet, a puppeteer is ready to give that puppet whatever voice suits its size and character—high, low, squeaky, trembly, forceful, or reserved. It is essential that the voice, once established, remain consistent, especially in terms of *pitch*. Also, in order to help the audience distinguish which character is speaking, puppets performing together should have voices pitched at different levels.

While developing puppet voices, a puppeteer should also consider diction, volume, accents, inflectional patterns and speeds of utterance. A tape recorder can be used during the experimental period to help determine the right voice for each puppet. It can also help in the evaluation of the show if the performance is recorded.

Once a voice is selected, the next task is to practice switching back and forth from a normal speaking voice directly to the puppet's voice. This becomes quite complicated and difficult when the same puppeteer is speaking for several characters within the same scene, as done smoothly by professional puppeteers.

Transitions from one voice to another can be eased if a puppet has a characteristic sound, word or movement that it performs just prior to speaking a line. For example, a puppet with a nose cold could sniffle, or an animal could make an appropriate noise. In addition, the same exercises that are used for choric readings and singing lessons can be applied to puppet voice practice.

For a comical effect, try giving a puppet a voice that is the opposite of the one that the audience would anticipate from the looks of the character. Remember, however, that it is equally important if not more so in this circumstance to maintain consistent voice quality using good enunciation and projection.

The voices of movable mouth puppets should be *synchronized* with lip movements. It is especially important that a puppeteer avoid "biting" words. Rather, the mouth should be opened on vowel sounds, such as the "e" in "men," or the "y" in "my."

The rate of speed of mouth movement in relation to the number of words uttered is variable. For slow speech, every syllable will be mouthed: MIS-SIS-SIP-PI. For regular speech, only two syllables would result in the puppet's mouth opening: MIS-sis-SIP-pi.

Experiment to discover how best to use speed, emphasis, and intonation to communicate the desired meaning of a line: WHERE are you GOing? Where ARE you GOing? WHERE ARE you GOing? Manipulate the head, arms, or whatever parts of the puppet body are needed to complement and animate the voice expression.

MANIPULATION

Any type of puppet should be constructed so that its character can be expressed through movement. Even the simplest of stick puppets can be built with eyes, ears, arms, hair, or a costume that moves freely as the puppet is operated. A puppeteer should experiment in front of a mirror to discover and then practice a range of puppet motions that contribute to the personality of the puppets and the action within a story.

STICK PUPPETS CAN FLY.

ROD PUPPETS CAN HAVE LONG, EXPRESSIVE ARMS.

MARIONETTES CAN RUN AND JUMP AND KICK.

HAND PUPPETS CAN HOLD THINGS.

Different types of puppets have varying capabilities and limitations in terms of puppet movement. For example, a marionette cannot easily clap its hands or pick up objects, but it can kick its feet and stand on its head! Mouth puppets with hands that are the actual hands of a puppeteer placed in gloves can become marvelous impersonators. A rod puppet's long, carefully controlled arms are perfect for expressively conducting a lesson or responding to music. In a group situation there is the added benefit that puppeteers of all sizes can work behind a stage and perform at the same level simply by altering the length of the rods.

A puppeteer can operate puppets from below by sitting or kneeling behind a stage. However, the movement is much less restricted when the puppeteer stands and holds the puppets directly in front or overhead. This added mobility permits performers to stay right with the puppets as they are manipulated.

An advantage of the overhead method is that it requires less floor space, thereby permitting a greater number of performers backstage at one time. Its disadvantage is that the puppeteer's arms can become tired rather quickly. This problem can be overcome, however, by having progressively longer practice periods.

EVEN A FINGER PUPPET CAN TAKE A BOW!

In addition to the above, there are a number of basic manipulation techniques and guidelines for puppeteers. These can be applied to the movement of most kinds of puppets when they are performing for an audience:

1. The operator should *look at the puppet* in order to keep it at the correct height (particularly in relation to any other puppets on stage), prevent it from losing good posture and eye contact with other puppets and the audience, and in general operate it convincingly.

2. A puppeteer should *maintain a consistent style of movement* for each puppet character. Bigger characters tend to move more ponderously than smaller ones. A dancer should *dance*, not simply bounce around on the stage. There should be contrast in the ways that different character types move.

3. Puppets should *move when they speak*, using broad, exaggerated motions that communicate the story ideas clearly, eliminating the need for extensive dialogue. Even so, it is sometimes necessary to include a statement about the action in the story. This can occur in the narration or within the response of another puppet: "Did you get hurt when you tripped over that rock?" instead of simply, "Did you get hurt?"

4. The puppets should make use of all parts of the stage. They can go in and out of doors, peer through windows, and appear at different levels, around corners, from behind curtains, or over edges. Sometimes it is appropriate to have a puppet come out in front of a stage as is commonly done with marionettes or story-telling puppets.

5. Puppet movements can become more clearly defined by having a puppet anticipate an action, such as by briefly stepping back before moving forward. This action is particularly effective after a puppet has been still for a moment.

6. Puppets should enter and exit from the sides or through backdrop and scenery openings rather than popping up and down. However, some performance styles and puppet characters can and even should use different ways to enter and exit. For example, a puppet can effectively convey the idea of climbing stairs as it comes up into view.

There are some manipulation tips directly related to the use of hand puppets:

- A variety of hand positions are possible; use whichever ones are most comfortable and offer the best movement for a particular puppet character.

- There are specific, well-defined finger, hand, wrist, arm, and body movements that should be carefully practiced and used to add meaning to the story line. This may include some careful handling of props and movement around scenery.

Additional ideas on puppet manipulation are contained in Appendix C relating to improvisation techniques. *Making Puppets Come Alive* by Larry Engler and Carol Fijan includes excellent guidelines with large photographs for teaching and learning hand puppet manipulation. Other books on how to operate and present all types of puppets are listed in Appendix E.

B. STAGING A PUPPET SHOW

Whether a production is to feature a variety show, talent acts, or a story, good showmanship will result if basic performance guidelines are followed. In addition to the ideas presented thus far in Appendix A, and to summarize ideas presented throughout this book, the following suggestions are offered:

1. Use *exaggeration* in character development as puppet motions and voices are established. A puppet is not meant to be an imitation of real life, but rather an *impression* of it.

2. In manipulating puppets and planning what they will do, take advantage of the fact that *puppets can do, say, hear, see and feel things that live animals and human actors can't.* For example, a puppet can swim in a river that isn't really there, or converse with an inanimate object. It can also talk without a mouth and cry without tears!

3. A puppet performance should be built upon *action* and supported by as little dialogue as is necessary to convey the meaning of the story. In most instances, *no one actor should speak for very long, and not too many actors should appear at one time.*

4. As a general rule, *the puppet or puppets who are speaking are the only ones who should be moving at that moment* in order not to confuse the audience. There are exceptions, of course, such as chases, mob scenes, or fights.

5. The use of *signs* and *props* in addition to *music, special effects* and good puppet manipulation will help get points across. Magic tricks, live music, and the use of live actors can also add variety to make a show more interesting.

MEANWHILE, BACK AT THE RANCH...

6. Make use of *audio visual equipment* where it will enhance the performance. For example, a scene can be projected from the rear onto a translucent backdrop from a projector, as discussed in Chapter Twelve in relation to shadow puppetry. A tape recorder can be used for special effects, or for playing before show, after show, or background music.

7. Props, puppets and other equipment should be positioned for efficient use. An act-by-act scenery and prop list should be posted backstage. Each performer or stage hand should know what to do, when to do it, and how it should be done.

8. During scheduled *rehearsal sessions*, the show should be practiced and its contents refined until all participants become confident and relaxed. The following ideas are ways that can help to make a show run smoothly.

   • When performing a series of short acts, several different stages can be used to eliminate scene changes and speed up the time between skits.

   • With a large number of performers, it is helpful to have them organized in order of appearance in a line extending back from one side of the stage, and to have them all exit as they finish on the other side.

   • Improvising should occur whenever necessary to keep the action going and in response to the audience and the situation at hand.

9. Considering all of the technical aspects of a production—sound, lighting, and special effects—*sound* is the most important. An audience will quickly be "lost" if a show cannot be heard, or if the pitches of several puppet voices are all about the same. After selecting the place for the performance, it can be determined whether or not microphones and a sound system are needed. If so, this equipment should be used for several rehearsals before the performance.

130

10. An entire production should be *short enough* so that the audience goes away wanting more. This possibility will be enhanced if the funniest or most dramatic idea in a series of events is placed at the end. Additional performances can often be arranged if the show has been well received, and if the puppeteers are so inclined.

11. How will people know about the show? Will they hear about it by word of mouth, a newsletter or notice, through special invitation, by reading a poster or newspaper article, or on a radio station? Plan well in advance what should be done, if anything, to *publicize* the show. It is generally a good idea to have a program outlined on a poster or chalkboard at the time of the performance, or to hand out programs. These are all good ways to involve group members who might not be operating puppets for the production.

12. Make sure the *seating* is planned or arranged so that everyone can see the performance. Before the show is to begin, sit on the ends of aisles or rows while someone else operates a puppet in all of the performing areas of the stage, and determine whether some areas or seats should not be used. In an auditorium, rope off those sections which do not constitute good seating. If adults and children are jointly attending, it is often advisable to have an area in front for children only.

13. Avoid last minute rushing around. For example, don't have the ticket takers also be the performers. *Begin the show on time!* If there are problems in setting up the show, delays can sometimes be prevented by having a repair kit handy.

14. Just after the show is over, the puppeteers should come out for a bow. Some performers feel that, if puppets are brought out for the audience to see and perhaps examine, it is best that these not be the same as the characters used in the production, as this spoils the dramatic illusion. However, in many informal settings, this is accepted, in addition to letting people come back stage.

15. No show is perfect. Every show should be *evaluated* with a critical eye, beginning with such positive comments as "I liked _____ because _____," and followed by constructive criticism. Based upon the performance and manipulation guidelines outlined above, a simple evaluation sheet or series of questions can be developed that will help in preparing for the next performance.

STAGES FOR ALL OCCASIONS

LAMPSHADE STAGE

NEST MADE FROM RAVELED BURLAP WRAPPED AROUND A STYROFOAM WREATH SHAPE

"TELEVISION" STAGE MADE FROM A CARDBOARD BOX

CLOTH BANNER WITH OPENINGS FOR PUPPETS, TO BE HUNG IN A DOORWAY

APRON WORN BY PUPPETEER & HELD UP BY TWO ASSISTANTS

A HEDGE FOR A STAGE

CARD TABLE ON ITS SIDE

"HOLLOW LOG" MADE FROM OATMEAL BOX

A STAGE IN A DOORWAY

LARGE STAGE MADE WITH TWO LADDERS AND A SHEET

PUPPETS IN A WINDOW

 EVEN YOUR ARM CAN BE A STAGE!

 BOOK STAGE

 MAKE A STAGE FROM A CAGE BY SLIDING OUT THE BOTTOM TRAY.

 FOLDING SCREEN

 BANNER ON A DOWEL, HUNG AROUND PUPPETEER'S NECK

 PUPPETEER STANDS BEHIND SECOND SHEET

TIE POLES TO CHAIR

MARIONETTE STAGE: STRIPS OF SHEETING STRETCHED BETWEEN POLES

 REVERSIBLE STAGE FOR USE WITH HAND PUPPETS OR MARIONETTES

 CARDBOARD BOX CHIMNEY STAGE

 SCENE PAINTED ON LARGE SHEET OF CARDBOARD WITH OPENINGS FOR PUPPETS TO PEEK THROUGH

 BACKDROPS

PAINTED WINDOW SHADE

SCROLL

CHALK DRAWING ON A BLACKBOARD

USE A SHOE-BAG TO HOLD YOUR PROPS

HAND PUPPET STAGE - REAR VIEW
Ⓐ SHEET TACKED TO POLE FORMS FRONT OF STAGE
Ⓑ PLANK BETWEEN CHAIRS HOLDS PROPS, ETC.
Ⓒ PUPPETS HANG FROM "CLOTHES-LINE" WHEN NOT IN USE.

USING PUPPETS IN OTHER WAYS

The contents of this book make it readily evident that puppets can be used in an inexhaustible variety of ways for many different purposes. Given or invented circumstances can be developed into planned performances based on events or themes from stories, life situations, or study topics. More incidental uses include teaching lessons, offering clues, greeting children, welcoming visitors, introducing activities, and so on. Whatever uses an adult plans for puppets, the decision should take into account the interest and capabilities of the group.

The following items are a collection of some specific uses for puppetry that are not already stated in this book. It is hoped that these ideas will spark new thoughts so that the reader, keeping in mind the performance and puppet use guidelines already stressed, can invent puppet uses that are directly relevant to specific needs in education, scouting, therapy, library, camp, playground or recreation work with children.

Community Helpers and Occupations—individual puppets are made as workers in a community, e.g. fireman, nurse, bank manager, fisherman, etc. Each child uses his puppet in front of a group to tell about his job. The puppet can then be interveiwed by group members. Brief skits between several characters may evolve on a spontaneous basis or with very little adult direction.

Map for Accumulative Story—create a road or map on several connecting or one large strip of paper, including whatever environmental settings that are appropriate. Puppet characters are moved along this map as an improvised or familiar story is narrated or told by individual puppet operators. A duck out for a walk could meet different characters and encounter problem situations. Stories such as "Chicken Little" are well suited to this technique.

Ralph the Reader—a large hand or rod puppet can encourage reading by telling how he eats up books with his eyes as fast as the Cookie Monster eats up cookies with his mouth (but he doesn't ruin them, and puts them back on the library shelf for others to enjoy). This puppet could be placed in a reading corner on a table or pinned up on a bulletin board, and could have a book jacket attached to its hands. When not in use, his head could hang as if concentrating on reading a book.

WHAT IS RALPH READING?

Book Character Puppet—someone who plans to read a story to a group might discover a story character that would make an excellent puppet which could be used to introduce, tell, and follow-up the story. As a child completes reading a book, he can make a puppet character to be used in book reporting or perhaps for developing a play based upon the story content.

MOTIVATING CREATIVE WRITING

If I were I would . . .: Introduce a puppet character, or refer to a puppet used in a puppet show or on television. For example, "If I were the Cookie Monster, I would . . ."

Situation Stories: Use puppets to act out part of an incident or the beginning of a story. Children write about how the story could end. (This "starter technique" also lends itself to good oral expression and role playing.)

Recording Sequential Events: After completing a puppetry activity, the child writes a diary or account of the steps involved, telling how a puppet was made, used, decisions that had to be made, etc. Each phase could be developed as a separate paragraph or chapter.

Character Development: Upon completing a puppet, a child could write about the puppet, using the format provided below as a guide:

Hi! I'm Fred Fiftyfoot.

My puppet's name is _____; I chose this name because _____ _____. In order to make my puppet I needed these materials: _____. The easiest part in making the puppet was ____ _____ because _____.

When I manipulate my puppet, I can make it _____. My favorite puppet movement is _____.

I like my puppet because _____.

Here is a special message my puppet has for you: "_____ _____."

The above format could be changed to have the puppet do the talking:

"Hi! My name is _____. I was made by _____. I like my _____. I can _____."

Of course, this approach readily lends itself to performance.

Handwriting and Spelling Practice—the puppet can hold chalk, a pencil, crayon, or even a paint brush and can write words, messages, draw pictures, etc. A puppet can dictate spelling words, or can misspell words which children will enjoy correcting. A puppet could also direct a spelling contest.

Punctuation Mark Review—stick puppet punctuation marks respond at appropriate times as story is read. Children can create puppet character on paper plate or plastic bottle, using only punctuation marks for building features. Then the puppet could talk about itself, using lots of expression to show how important punctuation is.

Listening Skill Practice—children manipulate puppets to act out a story that is read or heard on a record, concentrating on what the puppets should do in response to what is said. Puppets can be used to help give, interpret, or follow a series of oral directions.

Oral Language Development—puppets, props, story starter ideas, etc. can be placed in a puppet center where children are free to invent any use of these materials. Children might enjoy collecting and making things for this center, such as a small stage.

Group Discussion—each child has a puppet on his hand; this puppet does all the responding. Instead of the child raising his hand, the puppet raises his hand, or pops out of a box or cone. The adult leader would call on the puppets instead of the children for their contributions to the discussion.

Playing Games—a child plays a bingo or other game with a puppet on his hand; the puppet could actually be a player in the game, and have its own chance to roll the dice.

Word Study—puppets can respond to action words, read vocabulary cards, hold vocabulary cards for a child to read, take on the role of a vowel or suffix, or even a part of a sentence.

Special Occasion Puppets—these can be made for holidays, birthdays, or events. Christopher Columbus can tell about his voyage. A puppet can lead the birthday song and ask questions of the birthday person. On Mother's Day each child could make a "me" puppet to present to his mother, using a dialogue that tells all the nice things about a mother.

Mary Multiplier—this puppet can give out an "x" or a kiss each time a child correctly responds to a multiplication problem. Her features could emphasize the "x" symbol.

Who Am I?—a puppet can dramatize an event or situation and move in a stylized way to portray a specific character. Members of the group can answer such questions as, "Who was I?" "What am I?" "What did I do?" "Was I bad?" and "How do you think I felt about it?"

IMPROVISATION TECHNIQUES

These methods are aimed at giving life and character to a puppet by tapping the imagination of the puppeteer. Frequently good dramatic possibilities arise, providing a theme for a performance. However, the initial intent is simply to help puppet builders and operators discover how to convey ideas and movement through a puppet character.

Since it is best that a puppeteer learns to operate a puppet before giving it a voice, a good way to begin improvisation is through movement activities. Children will enjoy doing puppet motions as a group, each operating a puppet to the command of an adult director, or in response to the mood represented by music, or to actions in a story. Here are some suggested movements:

HIC!

- walking . . . leisurely, hurriedly, with a limp
- running . . . like a jogger, like a runner in a race, with an occasional leap.
- hopping or jumping . . . as if playing hopscotch or jumprope, or like a rabbit
- skipping or dancing . . . as to rock and roll, a waltz, or a Latin beat
- coughing, hiccuping, or sneezing
- waving good-bye, rubbing a hungry stomach, or playing patty-cake
- showing sadness, disgust, delight, surprise, anger, fear, drowsiness, shame, rejection, fatigue, amusement or anticipation

Once the puppeteers have explored puppet movement, a logical next step is pantomime exercises. These can begin with a single character, and then include two or more. The simple actions or skits can be outlined on cards which can be numbered to show easy to more complex situations. The book *Making Puppets Come Alive* by Engler and Fijan has many excellent suggestions for what to record on a sequential set of cards. Here are a few ideas:

- the puppet strolls onto the stage, looks down, becomes alarmed, then suddenly disappears.
- the puppet runs, falls down, gets up, and limps off.
- one puppet is on stage; another puppet rushes up, tells a secret, they nod in agreement, and bravely walk off together.

At this point the puppeteers are ready to add voices and act out situation stories. These can also be recorded on cards, and can begin with single puppets, then move to group scenes. Here are some examples:

- You have just arrived at the bus stop, but have missed the bus. What would you do?

- You are trying to work on a paper, but get constant interruptions from a fly. How would you react and what would you do to solve the problem?

- You are trying to sleep. Another person in the same room is snoring and restless, but you don't want to wake him or her up. How would you react? How would this other person respond to whatever you decide to do?

The use of a prop, such as a basket, ball, or watering can could be very effective in setting up a situation story. These types of events can often be worked in nicely with the interview techniques that are discussed in chapters one, two, three and twelve of this book.

Once puppeteers have gained some basic experience in puppet movement, pantomime exercise, interview technique, and situation story resolution, they will feel quite successful about carrying out a complete puppet play and will require a lesser degree of adult direction. Here are three general approaches for initiating the putting together of a puppet show:

1. A complete story line is provided from which a puppet play is developed; puppets are made as needed, as are props, etc.

2. No story line is provided; the puppet characters already made suggest a starting point or a theme.

3. A story line is partially presented, but is to be completed, using puppets already made or those that are created to suit the story ending.

If the group is large enough, it is interesting to use all of the approaches listed above and to compare the outcomes. In assisting with play production, the adult should provide tips on manipulation, voice, construction, etc. as needed. Appendix A briefly discusses these production elements, as do other portions of this book.

MORE PUPPETS FOR SIMPLE USES

WALNUT SHELL LADYBUG

PAINT HALF A WALNUT SHELL TO RESEMBLE A LADYBUG.

GLUE FELT TO FRONT HALF OF UNDERSIDE, AS SHOWN. WEAR WITH FINGERTIP INSIDE SHELL.

FELT

FINGER →

SEE-THROUGH MASK

BEND A COAT HANGER INTO A CIRCLE AS SHOWN, AND STRETCH A NYLON STOCKING OVER IT. GLUE ON HAIR & FACIAL FEATURES. HOLD MASK IN FRONT OF FACE. IT IS EASY TO SEE AND TO SPEAK WHILE USING THIS LIGHTWEIGHT, TRANSPARENT MASK.

TIE STOCKING →

FLY SWATTER STICK PUPPET

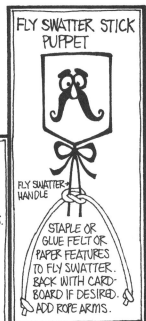

FLY SWATTER HANDLE

STAPLE OR GLUE FELT OR PAPER FEATURES TO FLY SWATTER. BACK WITH CARDBOARD IF DESIRED. ADD ROPE ARMS.

GLOVE SPIDER

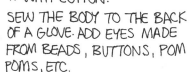

FOR SPIDER BODY, CUT OUT A 7" CIRCLE OF FABRIC AND BASTE AROUND IT. GATHER THE CLOTH INTO A CUP SHAPE AND STUFF IT WITH COTTON.

SEW THE BODY TO THE BACK OF A GLOVE. ADD EYES MADE FROM BEADS, BUTTONS, POM POMS, ETC.

SEW WOODEN BEADS TO THE FINGERTIPS, AND YOU WILL HAVE A TAP DANCING SPIDER!

GHOST ROD PUPPET

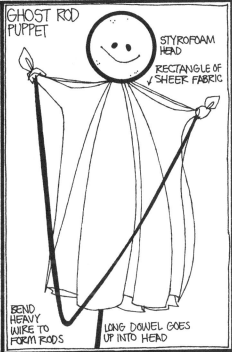

STYROFOAM HEAD

RECTANGLE OF SHEER FABRIC

BEND HEAVY WIRE TO FORM RODS

LONG DOWEL GOES UP INTO HEAD

BEASTLY POP-UP

SEW BUTTONS OR GLUE "WIGGLE EYES" TO A STRING DISHMOP

"CHOMPER" THE GIANT ALLIGATOR

HINGE TWO EGG CARTONS TOGETHER AND ADD A CLOTH SLEEVE. PAINT AS DESIRED.

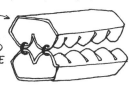

TO HINGE, → CUT OFF ENDS OF BOXES AND TIE OR TAPE BOXES TOGETHER

DRIED GOURDS MAKE FINE HEADS FOR HAND PUPPETS!

CARDBOARD ROLL PUPPET WITH POP-UP HAIR

STRIPS OF TISSUE PAPER TIED TO STICK

DRAW FIGURE ON ROLL WITH FELT-TIP PENS.

STICK PUPPETS FROM REAL OR ARTIFICIAL FRUITS AND VEGETABLES

INSERT NARROW SHARPENED DOWEL INTO HEAD. DRAPE CLOTH AROUND STICK AND TIE AT NECK, OR POKE DOWEL THROUGH HOLE IN CENTER OF CLOTH.

PUPPETS FROM STUFFED TOYS

CUT A SLIT IN THE BACK OF THE PUPPET; REMOVE STUFFING AS NECESSARY TO MAKE ROOM FOR YOUR HAND.

HAND

HAND →

MANY THRIFT STORES HAVE USED STUFFED TOYS FOR SALE

STICK

PIPE CLEANERS

STAPLE

PAPER TAIL

← STRING

STRING

BEADS

CARDBOARD TUBE MARIONETTE

JACK·IN·THE· BOX ONE·STRING MARIONETTE

"SLINKY" SPRING TOY

BOX WITH HINGED LID

DANCING STICK PUPPETS

PAPER OR THIN CARDBOARD BODIES, YARN ARMS AND LEGS

EGG CARTON SPIDER

ONE "CUP" CUT FROM AN EGG CARTON →

USE NEEDLE TO POKE THREAD INTO HEAD; FASTEN WITH TAPE.

POKE 4 PIPE CLEANERS THROUGH BODY TO FORM 8 LEGS.

FUNNEL-FACE MESSENGER PUPPET

CARRIES ROLLED- UP PAPER MESSAGES IN HIS NOSE

CUT OFF THE TOE OF A TUBE SOCK. FIT THE END OF THE SOCK AROUND A SOFT PLASTIC FUNNEL AND ATTACH WITH STAPLES. ADD EARS, FEET, ETC. AS DESIRED. THIS PUPPET DELIVERS MESSAGES AND ANNOUNCEMENTS TO THE CLASS.

PANTS-LEG PUPPET

USE A CUT-OFF LEG FROM A PAIR OF PANTS, OR SEW A CLOTH CYLINDER.

TURN LEG INSIDE OUT; GATHER & TIE ONE END SHUT.

TURN LEG RIGHT SIDE OUT; STUFF CLOSED END TO FORM HEAD; TIE OFF NECK.

CUT ARM HOLES FOR PUPPETEER'S FINGERS

INSERT A DOWEL INTO PUPPET'S HEAD. HOLD PUPPET LIKE THIS. THUMB AND FOREFINGER ARE "ARMS".

DECORATE YOUR PUPPET AS DESIRED

PAPER CUP PUPPET HEAD-CUT A HOLE IN THE CUP AND LET YOUR FINGER FORM THE PUPPET'S NOSE.

BLINKING PAPER BAG PUPPET DRAW EYELIDS ON BOTTOM OF BAG, EYES ON SIDE.

SIMPLE MOVABLE-MOUTH PUPPETS MADE FROM FOLDED STRIPS OF PAPER WITH FEATURES DRAWN ON.

DETERGENT-BOTTLE ROD PUPPET WITH STYROFOAM HEAD AND ROPE ARMS

COSTUME PAINTED ONTO BOTTLE

FELT HANDS

DOWEL →

MITT MUTT

USE A READY-MADE MITTEN OR MAKE ONE, USING YOUR HAND AS A PATTERN. ADD EARS, EYES, ETC. WIGGLE THUMB TO WAG TAIL. THIS PUPPET MAY BE USED WHILE SINGING "HOW MUCH IS THAT DOGGIE IN THE WINDOW?".

"TALKING" HAND PUPPET

MAKE PUPPET'S HEAD FROM A HOLLOW RUBBER BALL. USE A SHARP KNIFE TO CUT A SLIT FOR THE MOUTH AND A HOLE FOR YOUR FINGER. MAKE A PUPPET BODY LIKE THE ONE DESCRIBED IN CHAPTER 11 FOR LISA. PUT THE HEAD ON THE PUPPET AND USE YOUR THUMB & FINGER TO SQUEEZE THE HEAD, MAKING IT TALK.

CONTROL IS SIMPLY A LONG PIECE OF CARDBOARD FOLDED IN HALF LENGTHWISE AND STAPLED.

THE HEAD STRING SLIPS OFF OF THE CONTROL SO THAT THE PUPPET CAN NOD.

YARN TAIL AND MANE ADD MOVEMENT.

SIMPLE LARGE-SCALE MARIONETTE MADE FROM PIECES OF COLORED CARDBOARD LOOSELY JOINED WITH PAPER FASTENERS

"LEGS DANGLE FREELY"

RECYCLED WIG GUINEA PIG

GET A USED WIG AT A THRIFT SHOP AND SEW IT PARTLY SHUT AS SHOWN AT LEFT. ADD LARGE FELT EYES. THIS IS A VERY LIFELIKE PUPPET!

SEW

"CAP" PART OF WIG

PUT FINGERS INSIDE NOSE SECTION AND WIGGLE TO MANIPULATE.

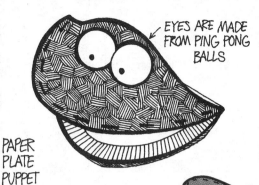

EYES ARE MADE FROM PING PONG BALLS

PAPER PLATE PUPPET

FOLD A PAPER PLATE IN HALF AND STAPLE ON TWO HALF-CIRCLES OF STRETCHY KNIT FABRIC. REINFORCE CREASE IN PLATE WITH CLOTH TAPE. ADD DESIRED FEATURES.

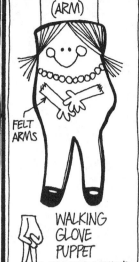

(ARM)

FELT ARMS

WALKING GLOVE PUPPET

← BACK VIEW OF HAND

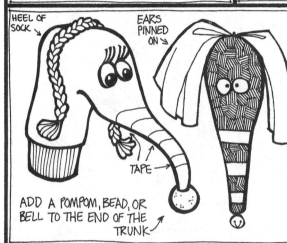

HEEL OF SOCK

EARS PINNED ON

ADD A POMPOM, BEAD, OR BELL TO THE END OF THE TRUNK

TAPE

"WOOZLES" ARE EASY-TO-MAKE SOCK PUPPETS. LAY A SOCK OUT ON A TABLE HEEL SIDE DOWN, AND FOLD OVER THE OUTER EDGES OF THE TOE SECTION TO MAKE A TAPERING TRUNK. WRAP STRIPS OF MASKING TAPE AROUND THE TRUNK TO HOLD ITS SHAPE. ADD EYES, EARS, BRAIDS, ETC. WOOZLES LOVE TO SWING THEIR TRUNKS IN TIME TO MUSIC!

PAPER CUP PUPPET HEADS, USING CUP HANDLE AS NOSE

"BIKE-HORN BEASTIE" STICK PUPPET

PUPPET'S VOICE IS DONE BY SECOND HORN ATTACHED TO ROD OUT OF SIGHT OF AUDIENCE ↘

ENVELOPE BIRD - THESE BIRDS CAN SING, AND THEY LOVE TO PICK UP LITTER! TAKE AN ORDINARY WHITE ENVELOPE (ABOUT $6\frac{3}{8} \times 3\frac{5}{8}$") AND SEAL IT SHUT, THEN CUT IT OPEN ALONG ONE LONG SIDE. INSERT HAND AS SHOWN; PUSH IN MIDDLE OF ENVELOPE TO FORM MOUTH. MAKE SHARP CREASES TO FORM EDGE OF BEAK, THEN FOLD THE ENVELOPE FLAT AGAIN SO YOU CAN COLOR IT.

SEAL THE ENVELOPE | CUT OFF EDGE | PUT HAND IN | PUSH IN MOUTH → | MAKE SHARP CREASES

PAPER PUPPETS WITH FINGERS STUCK THROUGH HOLES TO FORM LEGS, TRUNK, EARS.

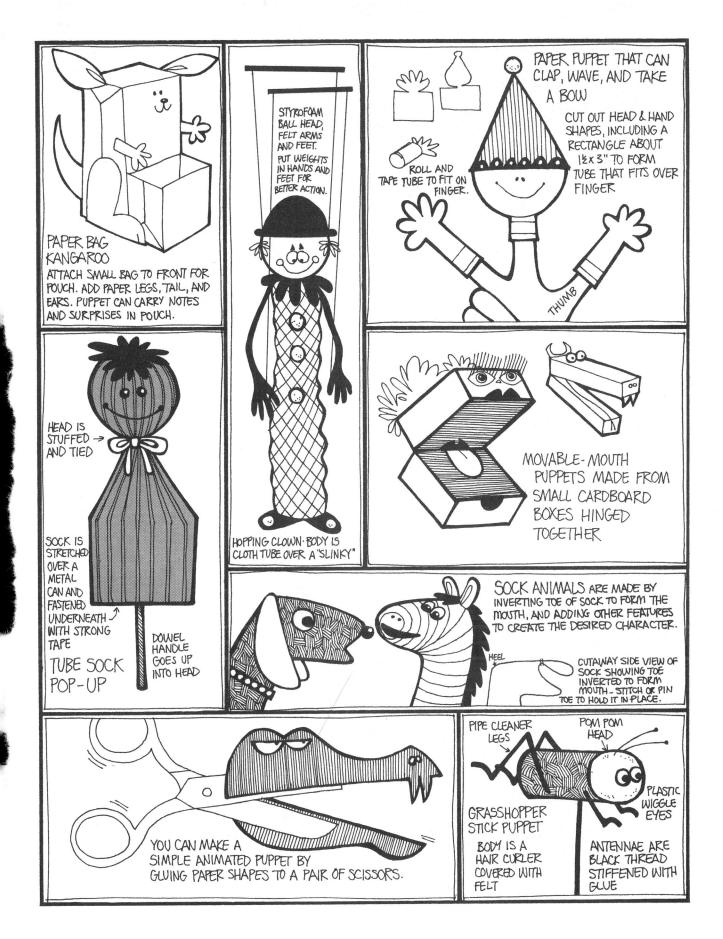

PAPER BAG KANGAROO
ATTACH SMALL BAG TO FRONT FOR POUCH. ADD PAPER LEGS, TAIL, AND EARS. PUPPET CAN CARRY NOTES AND SURPRISES IN POUCH.

STYROFOAM BALL HEAD, FELT ARMS AND FEET.
PUT WEIGHTS IN HANDS AND FEET FOR BETTER ACTION.

HOPPING CLOWN · BODY IS CLOTH TUBE OVER A "SLINKY"

PAPER PUPPET THAT CAN CLAP, WAVE, AND TAKE A BOW
CUT OUT HEAD & HAND SHAPES, INCLUDING A RECTANGLE ABOUT 1½ x 3" TO FORM TUBE THAT FITS OVER FINGER

ROLL AND TAPE TUBE TO FIT ON FINGER.

THUMB

HEAD IS STUFFED AND TIED

SOCK IS STRETCHED OVER A METAL CAN AND FASTENED UNDERNEATH WITH STRONG TAPE
TUBE SOCK POP-UP
DOWEL HANDLE GOES UP INTO HEAD

MOVABLE-MOUTH PUPPETS MADE FROM SMALL CARDBOARD BOXES HINGED TOGETHER

SOCK ANIMALS ARE MADE BY INVERTING TOE OF SOCK TO FORM THE MOUTH, AND ADDING OTHER FEATURES TO CREATE THE DESIRED CHARACTER.

HEEL

CUTAWAY SIDE VIEW OF SOCK SHOWING TOE INVERTED TO FORM MOUTH - STITCH OR PIN TOE TO HOLD IT IN PLACE.

YOU CAN MAKE A SIMPLE ANIMATED PUPPET BY GLUING PAPER SHAPES TO A PAIR OF SCISSORS.

PIPE CLEANER LEGS
POM POM HEAD
PLASTIC WIGGLE EYES

GRASSHOPPER STICK PUPPET
BODY IS A HAIR CURLER COVERED WITH FELT
ANTENNAE ARE BLACK THREAD STIFFENED WITH GLUE

ONE-STRING TURTLE
MADE FROM ONE "BUMP" FROM AN EGG CARTON. POKE HOLE IN TOP, THREAD A PIECE OF STRING THROUGH HOLE, TIE STRING TO NAIL. GLUE SHELL TO TURTLE-SHAPED PAPER.
WHITE PAPER REINFORCERS MAKE NICE EYES.

CUTAWAY SIDE VIEW

CHILD TAKING TURTLE FOR A WALK

BASIC SHAPE OF PAPER PIECE

ROD PUPPET FROM A TOILET PAPER TUBE
DECORATE TUBE AS DESIRED, ADD FELT ARMS, ATTACH THIN SKEWERS FOR RODS. HOLD AS SHOWN.

"TALKING" PAPER BAG PUPPET. CUT A PAPER CUP IN HALF; GLUE ½ TO SIDE OF BAG & ½ TO BOTTOM

MOVABLE-MOUTH PUPPET MADE BY GLUING TWO SMALL BOXES (THESE ARE MATCHBOX COVERS) TO A SPRING-TYPE CLOTHESPIN

A PAPER BODY MAY BE TAPED TO THE LOWER BOX.

TURTLE - STAPLE 2 PAPER PLATES TOGETHER AT THE SIDES. GLUE ON PAPER FEET & TAIL. PUT ARM THROUGH SHELL AS SHOWN. TURTLE HEAD IS A SOCK WITH TOE INDENTED TO FORM MOUTH. ADD EYES & DECORATE SHELL.

(CARM)
(HAND IN SOCK)

STITCH
CUTAWAY SIDE VIEW OF SOCK SHOWING INDENTED MOUTH

HANDLE FORMS PUPPET'S NOSE

BLEACH BOTTLE HEADS FOR LARGE PUPPETS

REMEMBER THAT LIFE-SIZE PUPPETS CAN WEAR "REAL" CLOTHES.

WOODEN SPOON PUPPET

MAY BE USED WITH OR WITHOUT A CLOTH COSTUME

GLOVE ANIMAL PUPPET WITH RUBBER OR STYROFOAM BALL ON MIDDLE FINGER

You're invited to a
PUPPET SHOW!

Date:

Time:

Place:

PUPPET SHOW

ADMIT ONE

PUPPET SHOW
• ADMIT ONE •

PUPPET SHOW

ADMIT ONE

PUPPET SHOW !

ADMIT ONE

PUPPETRY REFERENCES
PRINTED MATERIAL, OTHER MEDIA, AND ORGANIZATIONS

The books listed in the bibliography below are recommended by the author of this book and others who have found them valuable sources in puppetry work. Many of these books are not readily available in book stores. However, they are frequently found in college and public libraries or may be used on a reference or loan basis through puppetry organizations.

A wide range of puppet books may be ordered from The Puppetry Store, a division of The Puppeteers of America, 615 N. Bristol #90, Santa Ana, CA 92703. For a free booklist, please send two first class stamps to The Puppetry Store.

Books Which Emphasize Puppet Construction Methods:

Devet, Donald and Drew, Allison, *The Wit and Wisdom of Polyfoam Puppet Construction*, Grey Seal Productions, 1983. (a fun book with patterns on building human, moving-mouth puppets)

Dowie, Fran, *Big is Beautiful*. (how to build full-body and giant-size wearable puppets)

Flower, Cedric and Fortney, Alan, *Puppets, Methods and Materials*, Davis Publications, 1983. (a comprehensive book spotlighting modern construction methods)

Frazier, Nancy and Renfro, Nancy, *Imagination*, Renfro Studios, 1987. (using simple puppets to help children expand their ''imagining powers'')

Hunt, Tamara and Renfro, Nancy, *Puppetry in Early Childhood Education*, Renfro Studios, 1982. (easy instructions for teachers of young children)

Hope, Joyce, *Me and My Shadows*, Joy-co Press, 1981. (a teacher's handbook of simplified shadow puppet plays using the overhead projector)

Renfro, Nancy, *Puppet Shows Made Easy!*, Renfro Studios, 1984.

Renfro, Nancy, *Puppetry in Early Childhood Education Storytelling*, Renfro Studios, 1980. (combining simple puppets with stories in the classroom)

Roberts, Lynda, *Mitt Magic*, Gryphon House, 1985. (plays and patterns for finger puppets)

Rountree, Barbara, Shuptrine, Melissa, Gordon, Jean, and Taylor, Nancy, *Creative Teaching with Puppets*, Learning Line, 1981.

Scholz, Claire E., *Some Puppet Patterns and Stuff*, Dragons Are Too Seldom, 1981.

Warshawsky, Gale, *Creative Puppetry for Jewish Kids*, Alternatives in Religious Ed. Pub. Co., 1985. (using inexpensive, easy to make puppets to illustrate Purim, Hanukkah, etc.)

Books That Include Plays, Production Techniques, or Puppetry Uses in Education:

Boylan, Eleanor, *Holidays Plays for Puppets and People*, New Plays, Inc., 1974. (eight plays for Christmas, Halloween, and Birthdays, plus Aesop's Fables, and Punch and Judy)

Champlin, Connie, *Puppetry and Creative Dramatics in Storytelling*, Renfro Studios, 1980. (how to use puppets to dramatize thirteen modern stories)

Coad, Luman and Arlyn, *Producing for the Puppet Theatre*, Charlemagne Press, 1987. (covers many aspects of producing a puppet show)

Condon, Camy *Try on My Shoe—Step into Another Culture*. (folktales from East Africa, Mexico, Vietnam and North America, plus patterns for puppets)

Freericks, Mary, *Creative Puppetry in the Classroom*, New Plays Books, 1979.

Harp, Grace, *Handbook of Christian Puppetry*, Accent Books, 1984. (contains a great deal of information on how to present puppets in the church)

Korty, Carol, *Writing Your Own Plays*, Scribners, 1986. (teaches children how to write their own plays)

Marks, Burton and Rita, *Puppet Plays and Puppet-Making*, Plays, Inc., 1982.

Mazzacane, Mary, *Music Education Through Puppetry*, Keynote Publishing, 1984. (using puppets to teach children about music, instruments, etc.)

Merten, George, *Plays for Puppet Performance*, Plays, Inc., 1979. (contains eight plays for children of all ages)

Renfro, Nancy, *Puppetry, Language and the Special Child*, Renfro Studios, 1984. (innovative methods of using puppetry with children with various handicaps)

Rosenberg, Herlane S. and Prendergast, Christine, *Theatre for Young People, A Sense of Occasion*, Holt, Rinehart and Winston, 1983. (covers the fundamentals of theatre for audiences aged five through fifteen)

Schubert, Lettie Connell, *A Manual of Hand Puppet Manipulation*, 1980. (information for the beginner or advanced hand-puppeteer)

Schultz, Terry Louise, *The Organic Puppet Theatre*, Night Owl Press, 1983. (how to use puppets to teach children health concepts)

Sylvester, Roland, *Teaching Bible Stories More Effectively*, Concordia Publications, 1976. (how to teach Bible stories with a minimum of work or expense)

Guide Books with General Information on Puppetry

Lasky, Kathryn, *Puppeteer*, MacMillan Pub. Co., 1985. (describes in words and pictures exactly how a professional puppeteer puts together a puppet show)

Wright, John, *Rod, Shadow and Glove, Puppets from The Little Angel Theatre*, Salem House Pub., 1986. (covers the puppet theatre, theatre and stage, puppet construction, acting with puppets, etc.)